Focused-Driven Lifestyle Strategies

7 Strategies To Get Focused, Refocus, and Stay Focused in a Distracted World

Lyman A. Montgomery, MBA

Dedication

This book is dedicated to my sons Cameron and Destin, my siblings Robert, LyMartin, DeMeka, and Loveyah. I love you and thank God that I have the best siblings in the world. To my parents, Mom and Dad who taught us how to love each other and overcome any obstacles in our path.

Table of Contents

Foreword 1

Preface 3

Chapter One 23

Chapter Two 36

Chapter Three 61

Chapter Four 76

Chapter Five 87

Chapter Six 102

Chapter Seven 124

Chapter Eight 134

Chapter Nine 142

Chapter Ten 184

Lyman's Biography 187

Foreword

How interesting it is to find a book that will walk you through ideas to help you with focus issues and how to build your tolerance against pitfalls that will rob you of your time, lifestyle and legacy. "Focused-Driven Lifestyle Strategies" is written by Lyman A. Montgomery, someone who has dedicated his life to this topic and action steps.

Are you an entrepreneur? A business leader? Or in transition, if so, then this is the book for you! You may be someone who is wanting ideas to conquer information overload or strategies to deal with distractions in your life.

This book explains how to manage mental clarity, and your daily focus in order to accomplish what you need to do daily, so you can be who you desire to be or become in life.

I wish I had this book when I was in grade school as a launch pad to stay focused and gain more mental clarity.

A vow I made to myself many years ago was to maintain my focus and work on it daily. When I met Mr. Montgomery, it was exciting to know this was a top priority for him as well.

I predict as you read this book, you will put strategies in place to hone in on what focus means to you and how you will be working on it daily.

Do you ever ask yourself?
1. How can I deal with distractions?
2. What can I do to keep my focus on projects that have strict deadlines?
3. How can I clarify my mission on Earth through a focused-driven lifestyle?

As I read "Focused-Driven Lifestyle Strategies" I knew that if you followed the steps outlined and continued to repeat the process, you would be successful with what you want in life.

My charge to you is to get a handle on your focus, and you will have everything in life you desire. Enjoy "Focused-Driven Lifestyle Strategies" by Lyman A. Montgomery!

DAWN D. FOBBS, CPC, CPE
DAWNFOBBS.COM

Preface

Being focused is a great challenge in these modern times when distraction comes from all sides. But you should acknowledge that the sources of distractions, from mobile phones and the Internet to people trying to talk to you, are things that you can't do completely without. You have to make do with these distractions by learning to limit their impact on your life.

According to The Gallup-Health Ways Well-Being Index (2013) absenteeism accounts for 84billion in lost productivity. The Rand Corporation reported that each business dollar invested in corporate wellness expects to return $3.80 in savings, productivity, improvements and other benefits.

One of the greatest challenges of the modern world is to be able to focus. It's undoubtedly a world full of distractions, which may prevent you from starting a productive day, staying healthy and fit when the temptation of fast food treats and inactivity beckons, or enjoying the calm and quiet in the midst of a chaotic world.

Being able to focus will give you peace of mind, as you take on the world at your pace. It will help you simplify things and focus only on the things that will have a significant impact on your life. <u>Once you learn to focus, you will value the smaller things in life.</u> 🎥

You will become competent in handling things that life offers you. You will only spend time on things that matter, controlling wasted time on things that have only caused economic, societal, and individual problems.

You will learn more about focus, identifying things that matter, and valuing simplicity to improve your life. By focusing on small things first, you'll be surprised to learn that you're doing a lot for your life. Changing things for the better all starts with baby steps, from quitting smoking and eating healthy to being productive and being courageous in reaching your goals. You need to take on one change at a time, focus on it, and achieve it.

It helps to be fully devoted to the cause of finding focus by showing a willingness to make both minor and major changes. You can start small by clearing your desk, avoiding clutter in the office or at home, or testing the waters by disconnecting a few minutes to a few hours every day. When you're strong enough to focus for hours or even for days, knowing that you won't lose or miss anything significant for doing so, you would see the real beauty of a peaceful and quiet environment.

If you want to make an even bigger change, you want to help people find focus in their lives too. Start by telling them about how it's doing wonders for you. Then, show them how you're enjoying life now as a more focused person. If they refuse to give in, be patient and make do with the change that they can take.

As what this book will discuss, learn to go with the flow. Don't control the uncontrollable. Be flexible. Be strong in the face of distractions. Only then will you be able to focus and be a productive member of your home, office, and society in general.

Introduction

It was 2004, and life outwardly was great. I had a big house with a pond, plenty of money in the bank, a wonderful and supportive family with a growing seminar business. I felt life could not get any better. Remember that was life on the outside. Internally, I was distracted, unhappy and felt as if the world was closing in on me. I remember, leaving one of my sold out events, to return to the hotel and cry myself to sleep because I did not feel as if I was living my true self. Instead of a focused-driven lifestyle; I existed in a distracted-driven world where I was pulled in so many directions I could hardly enjoy the fruits of my labor. Can you relate?

It took missing out some great business opportunities and most importantly, missing a lot of family memories. The most painful was on my son's Destin's fourth birthday, I was out of town as usual working, my then wife had planned a birthday party and because I had missed other family gatherings did not notify me of her plans, about a day before his birthday, I called to say that I would be there and I got the shock of my life, *Lyman, I had not planned on you being there, so I didn't mention it to you."* Those words set me on the path to discovering how to get focused, set priorities, and become a better father, husband, and friend. This book takes you on that journey and shows you how to embrace and enjoy a focused-driven lifestyle.

Welcome to the Digital Information Age

While we take for granted much of the technology that surrounds us and the way it has revolutionized the way we work, live, play and relax; it's crucial to recognize just how much it has impacted our daily lives. Today we are constantly bombarded with information and stimulation, and it is taking its toll on our brains.

In fact, several years ago the average listening attention span was 20 minutes in 1980. Currently, it is about 7 minutes. When we account for active listening, it has dropped to about 8 seconds according to a study conducted by Microsoft
http://www.independent.co.uk/news/science/our-attention-span-is-now-less-than-that-of-a-goldfish-microsoft-study-finds-10247553.html

The Problem?

We're having a hard time keeping up with all this change! And it's leading to burnout. For a significant number of us, the demands placed on us are simply too great for us to shoulder. The constant stimulation and constant bombardment of information are leading to burnout. And knowing how to get what we want from life is seemingly impossible.

Our brains evolved in entirely different environments, and they just aren't designed to thrive under these conditions. The result is what we call 'overwhelm.' That means too much information, too much pressure, too much to do and too little time. We end up stressed, exhausted and disorganized, and it's just not good for our health.

Meanwhile, the expectations placed on us by our work have only increased as a result of greater productivity tools and enhanced connectivity. As my mentor and pastor said, *"We are more connected than ever before, yet have lost our ability to form meaningful relationships with each other."* And it's not just technology that has changed life for us either. The demands placed on us in other areas have also increased. The world is more populous; living costs continued to outpace wages and our roles in society have continued to change as well.

More and more women are now working full time, which while a good thing, has created new challenges in trying to raise and care for our children. I'm not suggesting that the role of women is to be the primary caregiver, what I'm saying is that our children have been forced to turn to technology and other electronic devices to provide comfort, instruction, and companionship that used to come from the family.

In fact, the roles of men have likewise become increasingly uncertain, and competition for employment is fiercer than ever. Don't get me wrong – none of this is bad in itself! Having greater access to entertainment, being able to communicate with anyone in the world and enjoying greater equality than ever before are all good things.

My point is, the state of the economy is a little less rosy, and for some, it is full of uncertainty for those struggling to gain balance and focus in their lives. Nevertheless, may I suggest that despite these difficulties and uncertainties, times are pretty good for those who are willing to live a life of focus.

Break Free from The Information Trap

If you're scared of looking ignorant, think about how many people will ask you about current events or laugh at you for not being updated. Instead, focus on the important things that matter to you. If you don't want to miss an opportunity, then control your need to stay up to date and spend your time on pursuing real opportunities instead.

If you're worried that you won't know the bad things that are about to happen if you ignore messages, you will still know. Family and friends will still tell you about an approaching storm, a possible economic collapse, or any significant event that might affect you.

If concerned you might experience something bad for not being informed; the opposite might happen. You can spend your free time being creative. If you're anxious, read the headlines of your favorite news sites, then tune out for two days before checking these sites again. Repeat this until you break free from the urgency of staying updated and enjoy your life more.

The Modern Dilemma
Perhaps this sounds familiar: You wake up first thing in the morning with a jolt because your alarm has gone off. In a rush, you brush your teeth and get ready for work while watching the news on whichever device you prefer. After getting ready and sending your love ones out the door, you set off yourself. However, there is a repeated dilemma that happens every morning; you struggle to locate your keys or decide what to wear, and 20 minutes later you find your keys or outfit to wear, now you are late again.

What follows is a tedious and frustrating 10-40 minutes of commuting – complete with other angry commuters, and probably a fair amount of time stuck in traffic. By the time you get into work, you're already stressed, and after peering at your computer screen for hours under artificial lighting, you have a headache.

You then have a cup of strong coffee, leaving you feeling wired, and you open your inbox to 10,000 emails (okay, maybe that's an exaggeration, but you get the point!). You spend the next 20 minutes on Facebook and YouTube watching cat videos and staring at photos of your friends on sunny holidays wondering what went so wrong with your life...

Lunch comes, and you feel like you've barely done anything. You head out for lunch and grab the cheapest thing you can find that's sugary and have another strong cup of coffee.

How can you be expected to progress in your career and to get the kind of lifestyle you want, when you're spending the whole time barely treading water?

By the end of the day, you've spent most of your time responding to emails and trying not to get distracted. You end up leaving an hour later followed by another hour of commuting yelling and giving the driver who cut you off the universal 'bird sign' with you middle finger!

You're now home at 7 pm. You should make a healthy meal for your family, maybe suggest a fun activity for yourself. But you're completely stuck for inspiration, so instead, you order a pizza watch television or Netflix and crash on the couch for the next hour or two.

The house is messy because you intended to do the dishes from last night, but was too tired and you realize that the laundry you planned to put in the dryer has mildewed and has to be re-washed causing you to feel anxious and stressed instead of getting any relaxation.

Yes, there were things you meant to do that were postponed, and the cycle reoccurs this evening too: intending to return the phone call from your friend who you haven't spoken to in ages, for example, was high on the list. So was paying that bill. Only you can't face the idea of paying that bill because you don't want to rummage through the piles of notices stamped "past due" on your desk. You're not even sure you can find the bill anymore.

Which would mean calling them on your lunch break to get them to send out another one? You haven't even looked at your bank account because you don't want to know how bad it is. You're supposed to be saving for a mortgage/your kids' college fund, but you have that party coming up that you can't afford but can't get out of either...

And you don't want to call your friend because you've now only got an hour left before you start getting ready for bed. And how can you justify calling that friend when you haven't paid the bill? So you avoid looking at the WhatsApp message because you don't want them to see that you've seen it; let alone spending any time with your loved ones.

Then you get an email from work reminding you how much you have to do tomorrow, which only stressed you out further. You browse Facebook a bit more and respond to some notifications from Candy Crush. Then you hit the sack – later than planned – and having done barely any of the things you wanted to do. You still haven't read that new book you bought three months ago and were excited to read. Maybe tomorrow will be a better day?

Except you can't get any sleep because you're stressed and you just spent the last hours before bed looking at screens, and the coffee is still in your system... And before the weekend, you have about 20 things to do and that party you're supposed to be attending. Can you relate to this?

Focus is about Assertiveness

Even if you are self-employed, you regularly work with others in the form of customers, colleagues, employees, and outsourcers. You can react in one of four ways: being passive, being aggressive, being manipulative, and being assertive. Being passive often means waiting for others to take action before we move on a project. This puts the fate of your project in the hands of others. The passive person has such low self-esteem that he either automatically agrees with others or runs away trying to avoid conflict.

Being aggressive usually, means that you move without considering others' feelings or ideas causing resentment. Aggressive behavior is competitive; the goal is to win over others. Being manipulative means getting what we want through devious means and making others feel guilty. It is indirect aggression. Manipulative people fear exposure if they are direct and feel it's safer to control and manipulate rather than confronting and being rejected.

Being assertive involves having respect for the people we work with on the job. It is rooted in high self-esteem and is most likely to give us the results we desire. We don't wait for others to act for us, we don't act without consideration for others when necessary, and we don't try to control and manipulate others indirectly.

Instead, assertive people negotiate to reach win-win results. It might surprise you to know that we all use all four patterns at times. These behaviors are established in us from an early age, and we may not be aware when we're using them. But with some awareness and determination, we can change these behaviors if we want to.

Identifying the best behavior to use in various situations can contribute substantially to the success of projects. The way to encourage assertive behavior in yourself is to:

- Be very clear about what you want
- Feel positive about your project
- Take initiative

Thinking through what you want and planning the steps might seem time-consuming, but the rewards are great. The way to successfully behave assertively with others involves:

- Knowing what you want and feel and be prepared to state that directly and simply.
- Maintaining your position steadily without giving in to manipulation or the negative behavior of others.
- Negotiate to achieve a win-win.
- Compromising to get the best realistic position is the right thing to do for the success of the project

Conquering Information Overload

Back in 1977 Noble economist, Herbert Simon warned about the negative effects of the coming Information Age by stating, that information consumes *"the attention of its recipients which creates a poverty of attention" (The Attention Economy, Harvard Business School, 2011, p. 11).*

Most of us simply have too much to do; we are too 'wired' and we are too bombarded with information, decisions and more. Approximately half of us are burned out because we're trying to do too much and because we're struggling just to keep afloat. The irony is that we end up achieving less the more we try and squeeze in, and as such, we can never get ahead. However, there is an answer, and there are ways around these problems.

The secret is developing a lifestyle of focus. It might sound like a small thing but staying focused is essential in today's noisy environment. By staying focused and keeping on top of all that information, those massive to-do lists and your calendar, you can take each challenge one step at a time. You can automate some of the work that is taking up the most time and energy; you can delegate, and you can find better ways to think about the problems and challenges that come up.

Focused-Driven Lifestyle Strategies

The key to living a focused-driven lifestyle is first, getting organized, second, setting priorities and third, learning how to control your schedule, so you can have MUCH more time for yourself, family and things that are important to you. In other words, you get to enjoy life again, while at the same time standing more of a chance of achieving everything you want to make.

The digital age is partly the result of all the computers and tools that are now integral to the way we work. So the solution? Start thinking and working more like a computer. That means being focused, methodical, organized and developing logical sequences. You'll learn all this and MUCH more in this book:

- How to reduce the number of decisions you have to make in a day?
- How to prioritize the most important tasks?
- How to schedule rest and recovery?
- How to save time by delegating and automating your tasks?
- How to keep your home more organized?
- How to calm your mind to eliminate stress?
- How to work more efficiently
- How to reduce notifications while staying connected?
- How to organize your thoughts?

- How to create systems and filing methods to help you stay on top of your work
- And much more!

Why it's Hard to Avoid Distractions

The difficulties stem from being addicted to your distractions. You are compelled to know everything and get in touch with everyone. But you can overcome your addiction one trigger at a time, so you can control each one better. Avoid feeling bored by pursuing a real passion instead of playing online games. Address your fears. Be honest what those fears are and confront them. Try to see just how real those concerns are by doing a test to determine if your distractions are real. You will likely see there's no ground for your fears.

How to Avoid Distractions

There are more sources of distractions these days with the availability of the Internet. Decades ago, people were only distracted by the phone, memos, fax machine, solitaire, and co-workers. Now, people have to deal with emails, IM, blogs, online forums, social networks, news sites, mobile devices, Skype, online games, online TV, eBooks, online music, videos, apps, and more.

So, how can you control the flow of these distractions? For one, you need to be conscious about how much time you spend online. Choose what you want to do carefully and focus on the most relevant information you have to offer.

Control Your Inbox

It's a common habit to leave your inbox open most of the time, at home or work. However, doing so will keep you distracted since every time a new email comes, you'll stop what you are doing to check it and even respond to it.

To avoid spending excessive time in your inbox, follow these tips:

- Make a to-do list out of the inbox. Read your emails and list down all the tasks you find in them. Do it on a Notebook, Notepad, or programs such as Taskpaper.
- Open emails only at scheduled times. Find the most convenient time for you to stay available through email. You could check your inbox 5 minutes every hour, or twice a day.
- Work without opening your email. Do this to all the other online communications and distractions too. Don't even leave your browser open to avoid the temptation to surf online.
- Prioritize your tasks. After disconnecting from your inbox, choose what's important.

Choose Your Responses

It seems like it has become a habit to always respond to emails, social network messages, blog comments, posts, and forum posts. However, this only makes you prone to distractions. But why do people feel that urgency to respond to things right away? It's mainly because of fear that people might think you're slacking on your job, fear that customers might abandon you, and fear that people will see you as rude for ignoring their messages.

Healthy Distractions

When thinking about distractions, you might consider them all negatives. However, distractions are also good because of the following reasons:

- They can give you a break. Distractions can relieve stress from your mind and let you relax.
- They can help you forget certain problems, pushing them in the back of your memory.
- They can inspire you, especially if you are distracted by reading articles and books, possibly giving you new ideas or a source of motivation.
- They can be fun and may even let you find new things to enjoy.
- They can help you refocus.

- Spare, a few hours of your day to focus on important things. Avoid communicating online.
- Follow intervals for work. Spend 40 minutes on work and 20 minutes for good distractions.
- Set disconnect time for at least an hour every day.
- Find more ways to balance your life between focus and healthy distractions. Consider your personality and needs as well.

By the end, you'll have more focus, clarity, and organized your life such that you can once again feel on top of everything and start making real progress. The best part? Instead of battling through the stress and hoping one day life will get better, you're instead implementing simple easy to follow strategies right now that can make ALL the difference.

Focus on Your Behavior

As an HR professional, I am trained to observe employee behavior and to help them make adjustments when their behavior does not live up to the expectation(s) of their job. When this disconnect occurs, they run the risk of ending up in a due-process meeting or possibly being terminated. The question is, how is behavior shaped? Your behavior is shaped by your habits which are directed by your daily actions (rituals), which begins with your thoughts. Throughout this book, I used the phrase, *"What you focus on EXPANDS!"*

As an example, I wanted to raise several million dollars to fund a youth program several years ago. I started with a simple thought (who could I contact to help fund this initiative?). Second, I formulated a list of potential funders or organizations that could partner with me (top 100 funders). Third, I began writing letters to supporters and completing grant applications; which led to establishing a habit as a successful grant writer and fund developer. Fourth, my consistent habit of writing successful grants helped to develop my behavior as a money raiser and launched my first business, *Innovative Funding Solutions, LLC* back in *2001*.

As you read through this book, and for the very best results, I recommend taking a single day (weekend) canceling all your other commitments, so you can reflect on how your behavior has gotten you to where you are today. Next, spend time organizing your tasks, develop your focus list, and implement new systems that will give you that "refresh" that you so desperately need. In fact, our company motto is *"Get Focused, Re-Focus, so you live a life with a focus."*

Once your mind is focused, everything else starts falling into place. You'll be more disciplined, more productive, happier, more efficient and less stressed. Let's get started...

Chapter One

Who Are You?

Before you put into practice specific processes for achieving your life focus, you need to do three things: first, be clear about your goals, second, understand what you say to yourself affects how you feel; and third, you need to have a realistic picture of yourself so that you can decide what you are capable of achieving.

Be Clear About Your Goals

One of the most important tools for organizing your time is to know your goals. When you know your goals, this allows you to prioritize things a lot more quickly. Know what's important to you, know where you're trying to get and know what you need to do to get there. This way, you can much more quickly decide what is most pressing and what will help you get there.

No one else can tell you what's important and what isn't. Not your employer, not your parents, not your partner. There is no 'right or wrong' way to live life, so you need to decide what's most important to you. Maybe that's your family, perhaps it's your fitness, and maybe it's becoming the next rock star sensation. It's all legitimate, and it helps you to focus your life much more quickly.

You may even decide that your goal in life is to have lots of friends and have lots of great adventures, memories, and experiences. In that case, you might choose to turn some of the advice in this book on its head. Maybe you spend less time at work and less time in the gym so that you have more time to fill your social calendar. Either way, you need to know where you're going and what's important to you.

What We Say to Ourselves

Do you know what you want? It's not always easy to know what you want because we are all told from an early age the things we "should" want. We hear about the achievements of others and their challenges and success, but we're not often encouraged to consider our strengths, weaknesses, and accomplishments. We can be overwhelmed by all the things we should be...

- Have more confidence
- Be healthy
- Be happy
- Be successful

- Get organized
- Be popular

I'm sure you can add your list of items. Added up, they can all make you feel like it's too much work and that you're just not smart enough or competent enough to successfully plan your life. That's the wrong attitude.

Why give up and underestimate yourself because of what other people say? Instead, let's take a look at who you are and what you have. We all have skills and positive qualities. Start emphasizing your good qualities when you talk to yourself and think of your weak areas as things you need to improve on instead of things you can't do.

Have you ever thought about why people put themselves down? Surprisingly, there's a payoff in it. People believe that it gives them the right to continue the negative behavior and not try to improve. So, how does that play out?

For instance, if you say you can't dance, people will leave you alone, and you won't have to learn, but you are angry at yourself because you know you're copping out, and you're envious of all the good dancers. If you label yourself as a failure, you can stop trying...but you're not happy about it.

What Others Say to You

Not only do we undermine ourselves with our negative self-talk, but there are plenty of other people willing to do it for us
with their criticism. Am I right? Let me tell you one thing that
stops you from paying much attention to them ever again. Most of the time when people put you down, it's because they're not feeling good about themselves. They feel inadequate and want to make themselves feel better by making you feel inadequate. That's all there is to it! Don't listen to them.

Here's the key. You can't please everyone...there are way too many people out there with opinions. Who should you please?
Yourself, of course. To do that, you need to figure out what you like and what you don't like. Then you have to start living
up to these demands. Below, you are asked to list what you like about yourself in the "Positive Picture of Me," which will help you define what's positive about you.

A POSITIVE PICTURE OF YOU

Think of all the things you like about yourself. Consider mental, physical, personality, talents, and abilities. List everything that comes to mind. This list allows for five, but I'm sure you have more.

1._____
2._____
3._____
4._____
5._____

Make a list of all the things you have already achieved. Again, it's probably more than five.

1._____
2._____
3._____
4._____
5._____

Make a list of people you consider to be friends, mentors, or "on your side."

1._____
2._____
3._____
4._____
5._____

Make a list of compliments you have received. (By the way, believe them. They were sincere, so accept them.)

1._____
2._____

3._____
4._____
5._____

Think of all the negative things you say about yourself – to yourself or out loud. Now, disagree with yourself! For instance, "I can't do anything." "No, that's not true. I haven't learned to do this particular thing, but I can and will learn it."

1._____
_____
_____

2._____
_____
_____

3._____
_____
_____

4._____

_____

_____

5._____

_____

_____

Defining Success

Now that you have a clear, positive assessment of your personality, let's look at your personal definition of success. Remember that success is fulfilling your potential in your own

eyes, not according to anyone else. For this to work, you HAVE to make a decision to change and understand that your past has nothing to do with your future and in fact, change can happen right now.

Before you can obtain success in your life, you have to be ready to take a focused approach to action. To do that, you need to define what success means to you in every area.

1. My personal definition of success is:

   _____

   _____

_____

_____

2. I will fulfill my potential in my career when:

_____

_____

_____

_____

3. I will fulfill my potential in my relationships when:

_____

_____

_____

_____

4. I will fulfill my potential regarding my health and fitness when:

_____

_____

_____

_____

5. I will fulfill my long-term goals when:

_____

_____

_____

What have You Learned?

Please write down what you have learned after reading this chapter?

Lyman A. Montgomery

Strategy 1: Direct Your Focus

It is said, *"With all of our getting, get understanding."* It is crucial that you understand that your focus has to be directed towards an object, idea or thing. What prevents this from happening are distractions. When you discover that your focus has been obstructed, you need to act  like an owl and consider all possibilities and alternatives in front of you. Through extensive research, I have discovered four common distractions that most people deal with daily: People (interruption); Process (poor organization); Product (tools and gadgets) and Psychological (mindset).

To deal with interruptions, especially if your work from home, place a busy sign on your door, leave a voice message letting people know you are unavailable during certain times of the day.

For Process distractions, find a system that works with your personality. When dealing with product distractions such as having the latest gadgets or tools, you should ask yourself, *"How will this tool move me towards being more productive and how much time will it take to learn and implement before seeing results?"*

To remove psychological distractions, release the things you cannot control and triage your thoughts into categories: *full control, some control, no control*, focus on the things you have total control over. It takes practice to adjust mentally.

According to Dr. Dahlkoetter, there are ten characteristics crucial for directing your focus:
1. Vision to allow you to unleash the mental power and follow your passion.
2. Self-improvement which allows you to strengthen the weak areas of your life.
3. Mental flexibility so you can stretch your thinking and imagination.
4. Self-understanding which allows you to know yourself and grow.
5. Balance in order to live a harmonious lifestyle.
6. Courage to overcome adversity, take a risk and learn from your mistakes.
7. Responsibility allows you take charge of your life and admit when mistakes are made.
8. Resilience to help you get through tough times.
9. Openness to learning lessons from your experience.

10. Enjoyment which allows you to gain pleasure from work and life.

Chapter Two

What is Focus?

You can search the Internet and find hundreds if not thousands of articles on the subject of focus, and each will tell you the importance of focus and what you should be focusing on to achieve success; however, very few articles explain what focus is? And why is focus so important? Keep in mind, whatever and wherever you focus your attention it will expand and grow; which means it is most real to you. Also, how is focus different from *attention* and *concentration*?

The Cambridge Dictionary defines focus as the *"main or central point of something; especially of attention or interests"* (www.dictionary.cambridge.org/dictionary/english/focus).

Attention on the other hand, according to the father of modern psychology, William James, defined attention as:
"the sudden taking possession by the mind, in clear and vivid form, of one of what seems several simultaneously possible objects of trains of thought" (Trends in Cognitive Science, July 2011, pp. 319-26).

In the movie, Star Wars, Jedi Grandmaster Yoda tells young Luke Skywalker, *"Your Focus is your Reality."*

Concentration is *"the ability to give your attention or thoughts to a single object or activity"* according to Merriam-Webster Dictionary. Another definition is *"intense mental effort"* (www.vocabulary.com/dictionary/concentration).

Why Focus?

If you're pursuing life as a creative person, such as an artist, designer, writer, musician, photographer, and similar professions, you need the power to focus. Distractions can ruin creativity in a snap. You can't create anything if you keep replying to emails, posting on Facebook, or reading a blog.

And even when you can switch between tasks, will you be able to do something effective? It will surely waste your creative time and attention, hence ruining your creative process. All the time spent on communicating with other people or entertaining other distractions is time spent away from your creative process. Being connected does help in encouraging your creative power, as you learn new ideas from other people and listen to their feedback, but you need to spend time on creating and building alone.

You can do that by making time for each process – for communicating and for creating. When you separate these processes, you can focus each time on a specific process. Your time for creating will be spent creating something, making you more productive. Separate your interests and savor the time spent for each one of them.

Aside from spending time for your creating process, you also need free time for the sake of your happiness, stress levels, and peace of mind. It's important that you be completely disconnected and experience real solitude. You can nap, write, run, read, listen, watch, or engage in quiet conversation with loved ones.

Now that we have defined focus and the two terms closely related and often used interchangeably: concentration and attention. We can examine four common types of distractions that hinder focus.

Distractions that Hinder Focus

In **Strategy One: Direct Your Focus**, I mentioned four different types of distractions: *People, Process, Product, and Psychological*. Allow me to explain in more detail how these distractions can affect your life and more importantly, how you can eliminate these distractions.

People Distractions (Interruptions).
There are people distractions such as dealing with constant interruptions, the kids wanting to play when it's time to study or work; not to mention, the telephone is constantly ringing. What about that coworker that stop by your desk or office to tell you about their weekend or asked if you saw the latest episode of some reality show? Before you know it, you have spent 15 to 20 minutes engaging in unproductive conversations without getting any of your work done.

Solution. Without being rude, let your coworker know that you would love to hear more about their week or the latest episode. However, you are on a deadline. Another strategy is to schedule time for what I call 'chat-time.' I plan about 5 minutes of my day doing this. When you schedule your day, people will respect your time.

For those working at home, designate a specific office or work times. I personally, place a sign on my home office door that says, "At Work." My family knows that when the sign is posted, I'm not to be interrupted.

To reduce phone call interruptions, place a message that says you are unavailable during certain times of the day, and you will follow up with them by a certain time each day. I also, suggest that you check your voice messages only during certain periods of the day (9 AM, 1 PM, 4 PM).

Process Distractions. (Lacking or No System)
Process distractions are a major problem today. What is meant by a process distraction is when your current process or method of doing something no longer works, and it creates frustration. For example, you used to pay your bills by sitting down and hand writing checks and driving to the post office to mail the check and waiting for the merchant to mail you a copy of your receipt.

This worked well until you get a new job which requires you to travel a lot, and you notice that by the time you get home you are too tired, so you put it off until the weekend. When the weekend arrives, you are busy catching up on the other chores you have put off, until you realize the Post office has closed.

Solution. A better process would be to pay your bills online or use an auto pay bill system through your bank. My point is that you need to assess if doing things, the way you have always done them is beneficial today? Another example is doing yard work. I know that it takes about two to three hours to cut my grass trim the bushes and clean out the pond. This takes time away from my family, so a better system was to hire a service to do this and free up my schedule.

Product Distraction (New Gadget)
One of my friends, Al is addicted to new video and camera products. His office is filled with products and gadgets he has purchased over the years. Here is the problem, about 75% of them are still in the box and have not been open. Once I was visiting Al, and I noticed that he had two of the same products on his shelf, I asked if he had purchased one for himself and the other for someone else? His response, "No, I forgot I had already bought that."

Sounds familiar? Are you addicted to every new gadget on the market? Are you still trying to figure out how to operate that "guaranteed" time-saving software that you purchased several months ago, but have wasted more time trying to figure it out, then simply pulling out an old fashion notepad to write things down.

Solution. You don't need any special equipment or software to be productive or organized. What makes this distraction is the fact that you are spending too much time trying to learn the software only to get minimum results, or it takes longer to load the software. If you feel that you need to purchase a new software package, find out what the learning curve is? Also, if you are not tech savvy, it may be in your best interest to go low tech.

Psychological Distractions (Mental blocks)
All of us have times when mentally, we are not present. Our focus is somewhere else, or maybe you just received some bad news prior to conducting a meeting or going on stage to perform. Psychological distractions are the most damaging because they are rooted in fear. Fear is a powerful emotion based on experiences collected and stored in your subconscious mind; which affects 95% of your decision making.

For example, you are about to go on vacation, and before catching your flight, there is a news broadcast that mentions that several people have been diagnosed with a rare disease found to be carried by mosquitos. All of a sudden you are filled with anxiety and begin to wonder, "should I cancel my flight and stay home?" What would you do?

Solution. In order to deal with psychological distractions, it important to acknowledge what you are feeling and to triage your distractions. This is my strategy. I will acknowledge my fears by asking, "Lyman, what are you feeling right now?"

Second, I will measure what I'm feeling against the facts of what I know. For example, I'm feeling apprehensive about doing training on a subject I'm not familiar with (fact). However, I know someone who is an expert on that subject; so I decided to ask my friend if she would be interested in co-presenting with me?

Third, I will tell myself, 'Lyman, I know you feel a certain way, but these people have come to hear you speak, and they deserve to have 100% of your focus. They expect you to give 100% so, put the distraction in the waiting room (write it down)." Once I'm done speaking, I will revisit the distraction. The key is to *acknowledge it, write it down,* and *deal with it* at a later time.

8 Common Barriers to Focus

While distractions are a primary obstacle to focus, they are not the only ones. Let's look at some barriers to living a focused-driven lifestyle.

1. PROCRASTINATION

It can be tempting to put things off by waiting for something to happen or letting someone else start the process, etc., but this is a lack of taking responsibility. The reality is that the longer you put things off, the less likely they will be done successfully. How many times have you finished something and said, "That wasn't as bad as I thought it would be?"

If procrastination is one of your problems, ask yourself why you are procrastinating. Is it a pattern for you? If so, can you tell if it's because of lack of confidence or if it's just something you don't want to tackle? Is there a common thread?

How can you combat this behavior? Can someone else help you to initiate it? Can you develop skills to combat your anxiety? Is it a project that you don't want to do and don't need to do, so the best course would be to drop it and go on to another project?

In chapter 3, I deal with procrastination at length and provide several strategies to annihilate procrastination for good.

2. ALL OR NOTHING THINKING

Sometimes life can seem so large that it is daunting, which can make it seem even more important than it is. Of course, problems can be broken down once they are understood; whether working by yourself or having others involved. You need to analyze the problem, set objectives, and then make a plan of action with a schedule. Review your results and make adjustments as needed.

3. FAILING TO SET A FOCUS

Some of us have a natural ambivalence to focusing, preferring to "live free," Being able to focus is critical to successful living and running a business. Research shows that the most successful people can focus and because of their focus they can achieve their goals. The secret is to set goals in a way that aligns with your personality and focus. There is an old saying, *"What you focus on Expands."*

4. FEAR OF FAILURE

Many people have an inaccurate idea that everything we attempt should be perfect, and that failure is embarrassing or

shameful. Of course, that's not true. Most of the time, we learn

a lot more from our failures than from our successes. We know

this but continue to blame ourselves. Some positive self-talk comes in handy here.

5. COMPARING YOURSELF TO OTHERS

This behavior has always existed but has become more prevalent in social media. Comparisons made in school, at work, and in social situations have adverse effects on our confidence. It can discourage us and even paralyze us. Again, logically we know that we're good at some things and not as good as others at other things.

To combat our counterproductive criticism of ourselves; we need to be reminded of the times we performed successfully. The only comparison worth making is comparing results. In other words, Did I achieve the results I wanted? If the answer is "No." Then use the result as a baseline to build upon in the future.

6. LACK OF SELF CONTROL

We all have heard people say, *"I need to manage my time better."* The truth is *you cannot manage time.* Can you add another hour to the 24 hours in a day? Of course not, then why do we say things that are impossible or illogical. Here is another one, *"I'm having trouble trying to make ends meet."* Think about it for a moment does the East ever touch the West?

The truth is, when you fail to get things done it is due to a lack of self-control unless there are circumstances out of your control. It's easy to give in to distractions and interruptions, which can result in disaster. Fortunately, developing self- control or discipline is a learned skill that can turn things around if you commit to it.

Self-control is rooted in your desires. Find out what those desires are and measure them against what you are focused on in life. Remember, whatever you focus on will expand. If you are determined to reach a goal, then devote your time to pursuing that goal.

7. LACK OF NECESSARY SKILLS

Sometimes, it's true – you lack the necessary skills required to be successful. The incorrect response is a lack of confidence. The correct answer is to identify the skills lacking and decide if it's worth the time and effort to improve, or would it make more sense to delegate or outsource. You have choices, and lacking a particular skill is not a dead end.

8. INEFFECTIVE GOALS

The final obstacle to being focused are weak or unrealistic goals. Too often, goal setting is more of a chore that we do each year, and for many, the results are lacking. A major part of focus is letting go or knowing what to say "No" to in life. Here are several reasons why 88% of people fail at setting goals:

- They are forcing you to work harder, not because you love it, but because you feel a need to set them each year.
- They might constrain and stop you from achieving other things outside of your goals.
- They might create anxiety and pressure to get all your goals done by a particular time frame.
- They might discourage you if you fail to get them done.
- They might stop you from living in the moment, as you keep looking forward to the future.

Instead of ticking off goals one by one from your list, you can do things that excite you. You can live in the present without worrying about where you'll be a few months or years from now. You can have the luxury of doing what's natural, not what's forced upon you by your goals.

And the biggest benefit of breaking free from the need to always set goals is to focus on the present and savor it. Simplify your life by clearing the clutter, taking it slow, going with the flow, doing things effortlessly, prioritizing things, and letting go of your goals.

Now, that you understand the most common types of distractions and how to eliminate them, let's look at some simple tips to overcoming focus obstacles.

Benefits of Disconnecting

You can do a lot of things when you're disconnected. It will allow you to enjoy the following things:

- It will give you the chance to focus on your creative process.
- It will help you regain your focus on work and other important things in life.
- It will reconnect you with people without any distractions.
- It will help you rest from the distractions of email, Facebook, Twitter, news, blogs, IMs, and more.
- It will increase your productivity and your sense of satisfaction.
- It will allow you to read books.
- It will help you to de-stress.
- It will give you peace of mind.
- It will give you time to reflect on life.

These are only a few of the things that you can achieve when you disconnect. So, how do you do it? Follow these tips:

- Unplug everything. Unplug your router, or disable your Internet connection.
- Follow a scheduled disconnection time daily. Set it for one to two hours minimum, and tell people about those times.
- Find a place without an Internet connection. You could go to coffee shops or public libraries without a wireless connection.
- Go outside. Run, jog or walk without a phone and enjoy nature better with your partner, child or friend.
- Shut off mobile devices. Do this when you drive or when you meet with someone to avoid interruptions.
- Activate blocking software to help you avoid distractions from the Internet, so you can't always access Twitter, Facebook, blogs, or other websites.
- Connect and disconnect in intervals. Disconnect for 45 minutes; then you reconnect. Connecting to the Internet becomes a reward for focusing on what you're doing.
- Don't bring your work home. Once you have logged out of work, make sure to focus on matters outside of work. Focus on yourself or your family instead.

The unfortunate thing is that staying connected seems to have become an addiction. But you can beat that using these tips:

- Determine your triggers. List these things down.
- Look for positive habits that can replace the old ones that served as triggers. If you quit smoking, you can take up running instead.
- Change the triggers, one at a time. Instead of opening your browser in the morning, you can get to writing right away.
- Find positive feedback for all the good habits you've practiced.
- Focus more on the positive feedback to reinforce your healthy habits.

Develop a Focus List

Now you have disconnected; the next step is to develop your focus list. The key here is not to make a vague focus list. If your focus is to lose 30 pounds by next year, then you are unlikely to be successful. Why? A year is a long time from now for most starters. This means you can put things off and hope that you'll be able to get back on track later on.

When we set our focus too far out, things outside of your control can interfere with it. In other words, even if you do everything right, you might not lose 30 pounds. This can be very disheartening and can lead to you losing motivation. So instead, your focus need to be concrete, short-term and well within your control.

A much better example?
"Go to the gym three times a week, every week" Or "Eat under 2,000 calories a day."

Develop a Focusing Ritual

Aside from making a habit out of disconnecting, you need to develop a focusing ritual. A ritual refers to a series of actions that you need to do until you feel physically compelled to do them. They become special actions that you need to do. When you have to follow a ritual, you can focus better and become more creative. Some of the rituals that you can try include the following: Spend your mornings quietly. Wake up before the other household members. Don't turn on the computer and don't go online.

You can learn more about my personal morning ritual by watching a sample video 🎥

Practice Focus Exercise

Do this exercise to make sure that you stay focused. Focus for 10 minutes, rest for 2; focus for another 25, then rest for

5, and so on. Concentrate on two things. You can do this when you have two major tasks at hand, but don't make the switch rapidly. Focus on the first task for 10 minutes, or focus on one task until you lose interest, before switching to the other.

Set a certain time to check your email or go social, then disconnect to focus on your creative projects. Reconnect for another period, then focus. Repeat this cycle. End your day right. Enjoy your evening by disconnecting. Perform a daily focus ritual. Review your week, look at your projects, edit your focus list, change your focus ritual to include only those actions that work, and review the rest of your professional and domestic life to see what needs changing. You can watch me demonstrating this focus exercise by visiting my Facebook Group Page.

Reduce Daily Decisions

John Tierney noted that *"No matter how rational and high-minded you try to be; you can't make decision after decision without paying a biological price."*

Once you become proficient at doing the focus exercise, it's time to look at reducing the amount of time you spend making small, unimportant decisions. These are time wasters, such as picking out clothes, deciding what to eat (as long as it is healthy and nutritional) and where to go to have fun in the evenings.

It is reported that Steve Jobs co-founder of Apple made a conscious decision to limit the amount of time he spent making small decisions, so he removed all variation from his clothing. He replaced all of his items of clothing with just black t-shirts and jeans. That meant every single morning; he would put on his one outfit and never need to worry about what he was going to wear!

Steve Jobs as you know, would go on to help invent the iPod, iPhone, and iPad. So presumably it was working for him! That's quite extreme of course, and not everyone is going to want to surrender all variation in their clothing. Thus, let's take a look at some more gentle and moderate solutions you can apply to your life...

What to Wear
While you might not want to go as far as Jobs with it, there are nevertheless effective ways you can reduce the decision making surrounding your choice of outfits. A primary cause of employees being late to work is not knowing where they placed their keys, glasses and the difficulty in choosing what to wear in the morning.

One of the easiest ways to do this is just to plan your outfits in advance (the night before) so that you have all of those items ready to go. You can even write this out in your planner for the upcoming week, like on a Sunday evening so you can refer to your plan.

What happens if you put on that outfit, and you don't like it, or you're not in the mood for it for instance? Another option is simply to have, say, twenty outfits for work that you know you like and that you know are suitable. Now, you can refer to any of those twenty outfits in the morning without too much thought. This is enough that your colleagues will only see you in the same outfit once every two months. Trust me; this will stop you from being stressed about whether your outfit works, or because you have nothing to wear.

Another tip is to ensure that you choose your clothes in such a way that they are combined into multiple different outfits. In other words, make sure that most of your pants or skirts match most of your tops. Now you'll be able to throw multiple combinations together with less thought.

What to Eat

While you might not want to keep your outfits the same every day, you might well be more inclined to keep your food consistent for breakfast and lunch. Let's face it; these meals aren't exactly 'exciting' in the first place. So why not have the same cereal and toast for breakfast each day and the same salad bar/lunch box for lunch.

As for dinner, this is something else you can plan at the start of the week. And it works even better if you can also prepare some meals – cook something big on Sunday and you can put some Tupperware boxes in the fridge for lazy evenings. Now you can reheat those meals in the evening, instead of throwing a pizza in the oven for supper.

And while you're at it, come up with some 'backup' meals that will keep. A good example is to keep a box of Mac & Cheese on hand for a quick meal that you can make in 10 minutes. I like to add broccoli to mine with bacon bits (turkey).

I know what you are thinking, *"Lyman I need variety in meals like I need variety in my life."* I get that; I'm just providing ways for you to limit the amount of time it takes thinking about what to eat. I've gone to lunch or dinner with family members or colleagues who take twenty minutes trying to decide what they want to eat. And once they decide, they spend another 10 minutes looking at the dessert menu unable to decide if they want the volcano chocolate cake or slice of Dutch apple pie.

Implement Themed Nights

Schedule some of your daily activities to reduce decision fatigue by making each night of the week a "theme night." So Monday can become 'Couch Potato night' where you're allowed to watch TV without the guilt. Tuesday can become 'Date Night' where you commit yourself to spend some quality time with your other half. Wednesday can become 'Chores night' where you clean the house or do laundry.

As a child, my family dedicated Thursday as "Family Night." All of the kids would serve as entertainment, my brother Robert would sing, I would give a speech or recite a poem, my younger brother, LyMartin would dance, and my sister, DeMeka would talk about Math (She's a CPA today).

By doing this each evening, you remove the stressful need to make that "right decision." This way, you can stay on top of things without feeling emotionally drained and frustrated.

I hope that these tips provided in this chapter will help you to **simplify** your life. There are more methods you can use to do this as well, so start putting them into action and just reduce the number of decisions you have to make. To help you do this, list some things that you can do to plan your life better and simplify your decision-making time?

Now that we have defined focus, common hindrances and obstacles to focus and tips for overcoming these barriers; we can turn our attention to how energy and motivation drive focus.

Energy Drive Focus

Have you ever experienced a mental blur? Mental blurs cause us to be out of focus due to not having enough energy to keep you alert. This mental blur is also known as mental fatigue and fogginess. That is why energy management is much more important than so-called time management. A HUGE component of energy management is to understand the impact that decision making has on our energy levels. Every time you have to make a decision, this takes a toll on your energy levels and leaves you with a little less energy to 'spend' on other tasks.

For instance, when you wake up in the morning and decide what you're going to wear, that will not only take up time, but it will also take up energy. Likewise, when you choose what to have for lunch, you'll also be using up your mental energy to make that decision.

And this then means that you have less energy when it comes to making other, more important decisions. When someone asks you what to do at work, or when you're wondering how best to save your money, you now have less mental energy available to dedicate to that decision. By the end of the day, you burn out!

To begin, many think that the biggest 'limit' on our ability to get things done is a lack of enough time. We all make the excuse that we don't exercise because we don't have time and that we don't do more with the family because we don't have time. That's not true. If you think back to all of those times in your life when you've been doing 'nothing,' then you'll probably realize that you had plenty of time.

Just this week, you've probably spent at least a good couple of hours on Facebook/YouTube/the website of your choice, and there's a good chance you've watched a fair amount of useless TV as well. During this time, you could have been exercising, returned your friend's phone call, and cleaned the house.

What's the point?
Your energy tank is low or depleted, and you are in need of recharging your energy cells. Did you know that your willpower decreases as your energy tanks run low or are exhausted? Not only do you have the less physical energy to get up and complete house chores, when you're tired, you

also have less mental willpower to encourage yourself to do it.

Motivation Drive Focus

While energy drives focus, motivation is one of the most important ingredients in staying focused. Doesn't it make more sense that your project or business will be more successful if you want to do it? It is your motivation that takes you a long way when you're trying to make changes to your behavior. Many people want to accomplish a certain thing, but can't get started, or they lose steam as time progresses.

What Have You Learned?

As I end this chapter, write down what you have learned and will implement today?

_____

_____

_____

_____

_____

Chapter Three

Focus Destroys Procrastination

Procrastination if left unchecked can turn into a bad habit which could eventually be very hard to break. In my home office, I have a slogan that I keep on my wall that says, "Accept No Excuses, Only Results." You may not realize that the habit of procrastination can cost you a lot of negativity; therefore, you should take the time to identify and eradicate this element.

The following are some of the most popular excuses why people lapsed into the procrastination habit:

- The famous "I don't know" excuse. This is one of the most popular excuses given when you are not interested in getting a particular task done.

- Not challenging enough. This is another poor excuse often given as a way out of getting something done.

- Not feeling like it. This is plain and simple laziness, but it will not be acknowledged as such.

- Cannot be forced – eventually, when all else fails, you resort to this argument, whereby some level of hostility is injected into the situation. If used often enough this aggressive behavior can have even more damaging results, as you learn to rely on this negative element to get out of doing things.

Although procrastinators are capable of using every excuse in the book, there are compelling underlying influences that can cause you to procrastinate. Exploring these contributing factors may allow you to break this negative cycle. Here are some common fears associated with procrastination.

Common Fears

Before you can face your fears, it's important to understand that fear is based on the stories you continue to tell yourself. Here is what I mean. You grew up in a household where your parent demanded perfection at all time. You had to maintain a certain grade point average or you "were lazy and stupid."

As a result, you believe that if you are not perfect, then you are stupid and lazy. In reality, what has happened is what I call the **F.I.S.T** principle: Facts are Interpreted based on the

Stories we tell ourselves until we acknowledge and accept the Truth.

Here is another example of the **F.I.S.T** principle: A person has a cough and nasal congestion (**Facts**). You begin to think, my father had a similar cough and was diagnosed with lung cancer (**Interpretation**). Maybe that's what wrong with me; I have cancer because I used to be a smoker for five years (**S**tory). You finally go to the doctor, and it turns out, you had a common cold with congestion (**Truth**).

Now that you see how the **F.I.S.T** principle keeps you in fear and promotes procrastination; fears that contribute to promoting procrastination are:

Fear of failure – sometimes even the hint of possible failure can effectively keep you from even wanting to make an attempt at a particular task. This failure is perceived to be crippling both mentally and physically as you seem to be terrified of having to face such a possibility. This could be due to many connecting factors; one of which could be the need to be and look accomplished and successful always.

Fear of painful outcomes – this too can keep you from trying new things or even getting anything done at all. This could stem from a bad experience in which you have not come to terms with, therefore conveniently using this particular excuse is a good way to inject procrastination into the equation. Although this can sometimes be very real, using this as a pretext, will not help you in future endeavors, neither will it help to build good character.

Fear of missing out – Do you feel like you need to do everything and be everywhere? If so, you could turn into a person who eventually resorts to procrastination as a defense mechanism. This usually happens when you have a "go getter" mindset, which works to a certain point until mental and physical exhaustion set in and you decide to quit.

Procrastinators Love Their Comfort Zones

Most people who consciously want to avoid working on a task, in a group or project will usually form some sort of comfort zone. This often will be difficult to rationalize. However, understanding the connections between the security comfort zones provide and the actual procrastination will allow you to manage the situation better.

One of the more popular comfort zones is hiding behind the phrase, "I don't know." By giving this type of answer for anything, it almost always deters any follow-up actions or comments from others; thus effectively keeping you from having to deal with conflict or finding solutions.

Another popular excuse used as a comfort zone is a lack of supporting tools for the job. A lot of people use this as a great excuse for not wanting to do anything they don't desire to do.

A favorite procrastination comfort zone lies in the expression of not being able to cope with a particular situation. This comfort zone disallows you from making any attempt of trying to complete a task, as perceived failure is dominant and crippling your thinking. Therefore, a buffer is set up against any possible harm perceived to be imminent.

Procrastination is about Perspective

For some, procrastination is keen to laziness, but for those who are committed to understanding this particular mindset, procrastination goes much deeper and is more complicated than simple laziness. The following are some ways you can control and eventually eradicate this debilitating disease:

As a lot of procrastination actions begin with your perspective of the situation, this is an ideal place to start. Putting down on paper all the things that should be done to this date and time, that have not been attempted should be the first things that go into the list.

In doing so, you are taking the responsibility to recognize some of the things that require your attention. When this happens, there is no real excuse, only results. Going over the list, and then identify at least one thing that can be attempted should ideally be the next course of action.

This should be followed with a complete and relevant plan which will effectively help to complete the task chosen. Once the plan is well mapped out, you have no further excuse to delay action. Ideally, the plan should cover all possibilities to keep you from defaulting and abandoning the plan format.

A specific time frame should be allotted, and this should be done without any room for wavering in the decision. This time frame should be the focus of the entire exercise to get the chosen task done. You have to be willing to commit to adhering the time frame stipulation allotted. This will create an effective check and balance scenario.

Write What You Are Feeling
In chapter 9, I will provide you with a 30 Day challenge to journal your thoughts and emotions. In this section, I will introduce the concept of creating a journal. Starting a journal maybe one action that allows you to face procrastinating challenges and acknowledge the hold it has on your life. The following are some areas that should ideally

be covered by the journal to ensure its effectiveness both physically and mentally:

- Starting a journal would require total honesty on the part of you. With total honesty, you should list down the entire amount of tasks that you have consciously avoided or didn't complete in the past. Nothing should be considered too insignificant and unnecessary; neither should you resort to only documenting tasks that were considered a challenge only.

- Once this is done, you should note, in a column beside each task, the reason the task was abandoned or not completed to date. Documenting this reason will give you a chance to consider the relevancy of the excuse used, to avoid doing or completing the task. Only then will you be able to understand the extent you are willing to go to avoid the task.

- Once this is acknowledged, you can then move on to documenting every task eventually carried out and completed as they unfold. This is a great motivating tool, especially when you begin to tackle more tasks as your confidence levels grow and the procrastinations decrease.

Use Your Body Against Procrastination

It is popularly thought that the mind is the dominant factor in allowing the procrastinating attitude to prevail in one's life. However, there is also the contribution of the body to this equation, as it responds to what the mind dictates. Realizing the mind is still the dominant factor, the body can be motivated to overcome this thought process and keep procrastination at bay.

The following are some ways the body can be used to break the procrastination mindset:

- ✓ Finding the best time to work on a particular task helps the body to be more willing and energized to see tasks completed. If there are no distractions and the body is relaxed, the chances are better for successful completion of tasks.

- ✓ Given the uniqueness of your work habits and the way the body responds, it would be a worthwhile effort to stop and consider the circumstances in which your body is most likely to respond positively to working on something to its completion.

- ✓ Although multi-tasking is something that most people think they are capable of doing effectively; research shows that this is not true. When it comes to multi-tasking, it would be better for the body to focus on getting one thing done at a time or working in stages with concentrated effort.

- ✓ Overestimating a particular task would also not work well when it comes to getting the cooperation of the body. Tiredness both mentally and physically is very likely to dominate, thus giving you an ideal excuse to abandon the task. Therefore, careful consideration should be given to ensure your body is capable of handling the task.

Reprogramming Your Brain

In order to overcome these fears, you must reprogram your thinking. New research has been able to show that there are many practical ways the mind can be "taught" not to give in to the urge to procrastinate.

With this research, many procrastinators have attested to being able to beat this often debilitating habit. The following are some of the ways recommended, and often adopted by those who were able to control the procrastination mindset effectively:

- Making a firm commitment – when the mind is conditioned to adhere to certain criteria, it will function accordingly. Using the commitment as a firm indicator of what is expected, the individual will be able to focus the mind and program the brain on carrying out the task based on the commitment given.

- Another way of programming the brain not to indulge in procrastination would involve removing distractions from your working environment. These distractions are always the elements that provide the individual with a loss of focus and affect the delivery time of a project. Distractions are also always the excuse the individual gives for not being able to stick to the task and schedule.

- Setting realistic goals and having the added incentive of a reward system that is both pleasing and attainable would be another way to train the brain to evade procrastination.

The goals will give you a clear picture of what the end results should be like, and incentives will help to keep your focus steady and unwavering. Effectively ensuring the task is completed within the initially designated time frame and according to specifications. Taking time to design incentives that are attractive is better than just throwing together just any types of rewards.

Techniques to Annihilate Procrastination

When you remove the procrastination mindset, several adjustments should be made. There are many ways to go about curbing the procrastination bug, but all of them ideally need your cooperation and willingness.

One of the more effective ways of overcoming the first instinct to procrastinate would be to design the task to ensure it does not seem overwhelming. This overwhelming element usually births the natural instinct to shy away from the task hence the choice to procrastinate. Breaking the tasks into smaller and more manageable sections would then ideally give you a chance to try and tackle one part at a time.

Sometimes and improvement or a complete change in the working environment will help you be more comfortable both in body and mind, and thus be better able to cope with tasks presented. These changes need not be very drastic or monetarily high. A few small adjustments and the addition of color sometimes can brighten the work environment enough to get you out of the rut and productive again.

Maintain a positive mindset, by reading such material or motivating oneself with audio and visual stimulations will help you be more focused and result driven. Motivation can urge you to take the necessary actions to ensure tasks are done.

Positive thinking always helps and push you to explore further and get more things done without the negative existence of procrastination.

Energy and behavior patterns have a lot to do with your mental and physical state, and this is a very dominating feature that dictates your general capability levels. There are a lot of ways to ensure you are ready to make a decision that keeps the procrastination mindset in check.

The following are tips to annihilate procrastination before it takes over, become a habit and destroys your credibility:

- o Start with some good habit forming actions, such a picking a couple of items to be completed before actually launching oneself into the work routine of the day. When these tasks have been identified, focus on immediately getting it done. Once this becomes a daily routine and a habit, you will be able to reflect on

- Boosting the energy levels to cope with the daily demands on the mind and body should also be a daily regimen consideration. Eating healthy and having a good exercise regimen will benefit both the mind and body and keep you alert and ready to face the challenges of the day.

- Getting into the habit of doing things immediately as they pop up, is something the most focused individuals are capable of doing successfully. Building on this positive trait will help to ensure procrastination is removed from your life. Once accomplished, you will stay on top of your game.

What Have You Learned?

Write down which techniques you will use to annihilate your procrastination?

_____
_____
_____
_____
_____
_____
_____

Strategy 2: Focus on Teamwork

The second strategy is to work as a team. When I work with clients on developing their focus, I will ask them to work with someone who can hold them accountable and let them know if they are getting off course. Research has shown that people get more done and sustain their goals longer when they work as a team. Other than dividing up the workload, working as a team to get focus allows you to get another perspective from someone else's point of view. I can remember thinking I was heading in the right direction with a proposal until my business partner reviewed it and noticed I had accidentally omitted a significant segment of the project.

The point I'm making is that we cannot always see our blind spots. Jack Canfield, Mark Victor Hansen, and Les Hewitt provide a great action plan for success in their book, The Power of Focus. Here are several steps that you and your team should incorporate:

1. What is/are your challenges?

2. Make a decision to confront issues and deal with them.
3. What's the desired result?
4. How will you/team feel when issue(s) is/are resolved.
5. What information do we need to resolve issues?
6. What can I/we do to make a difference?
7. What action will I/we take today?
8. When will I/we set a time and date to follow-up?

Chapter Four

Build a Focused Team

It is strongly recommended that you hire a coach or consultant to help you in areas where you are not strong. The difference between Coaches (life and business). A life coach will help you get your life in order to match your desires as a person and realize the things you may need to release to grow.

Hire a Coach

A coach will guide you along your professional path and discover your talents based on your focus, whether it be business, health, or in life. It is my experience that you need both a personal life coach and business coach because both are necessary. Here is why? Your personal life will interfere with business and business dealings will interfere you're your personal life. Do yourself a favor and work on the whole of you.

Consultant/Contractor

A consultant will give you the guidelines to make you more successful at completing tasks to get you closer to your goals and even share new ideas to give you more fuel to propel forward. A contractor will lay out the plans and tackle each one for you without you being present. They have the expertise, resources, and know-how while you are responsible for paying them and working with their deadlines.

Who is on Your Team?

When it comes to employment, the first question to ask yourself is "Will I do it or hire a service?" For instructions on how to contract 1099 workers, please check your State and Federal laws. Here is a checklist to make sure you only hire team members that support your vision and are willing to make it a reality:

- Only work with those who love your vision and are willing to move it forward. Over the years I have hired thousands of employees as a Human Resources professional, and there have been times when I have had to terminate a worker's employment because they did not adhere to the policies or just did not fit the culture and resigned their position.

- I can tell you with confidence that in most cases which resulted in terminations or resignations, the employee refused to advance the vision of the organization. It is imperative that you master the art of interviewing and selecting the best-fit person to be on your team.

- Hire people who speak your business language. Every industry has its acronyms and jargons that are unique. Likewise, you should make sure that you hire staff that understands your specific jargon and can represent your brand.
- Provide training and education on the vision of the company to ensure all team members are focused daily. You will decide how often team building exercise will take. For example, in some companies, they do morale boosting activities on early morning calls or at the work site before the daily grind of work begins.

- Use webinars or assign daily motivational videos for your employees to look at and comment on the training.

- Use a discussion box for improvements. Remember, whoever makes the suggestion will have to own it and back up any ideas you think supports it. Make it fun and reward great ideas or suggestions.

- Model your process and see to it the team follows your great examples. Have the mission and vision placed in areas where people see it daily? Your mission and vision should be short and sweet enough that it will fit on a t-shirt.

To keep your team focused, I suggest that you hold weekly "pit stop" meetings that only last 7 minutes, and it's a time to ask three critical questions:

1. What are you currently focusing your time and energy on (project)?
2. How is the project going?
3. How can I assist you in getting your project or task completed?

Here are several key factors that *performing* and *non-performing* teams have in common. Functional-performing teams tend to be:

- **D**ynamic
- **R**elational
- **E**fficient
- **A**ctive
- **M**otivated

Did you notice that performing teams spell out the word **DREAM**? Functional-performing teams are dynamic in their formation; each member understands that they each bring a different perspective to the team and collectively they can achieve a common goal. These teams are also relational in the context that they feed off each other's ideas, and there tends to be a synergy created.

Perhaps the greatest attribute of functional-performing teams is their efficiency. They can reduce things down to its common denominator and assign tasks to individuals based on their skill or expertise, as well as desire.

Another aspect of functional performing teams is that they are active in their pursuit of excellence. They take pride in their work and are willing to work hard and together to achieve their goals.

Lastly, they are motivated by a passion and innate desire to excel and go beyond meeting a deadline. They will set the bar high and exceed expectations.

In direct contrast, *Dysfunctional Non-performing* teams tend to be:
- **M**onotonous
- **O**verworked
- **B**urnout

Dysfunctional Non-performing teams have a tendency to act as a mob by being monotonous in their approach to solving problems; they may seek constant guidance and feedback before taking the initiative to get started. Many have had bad experiences with teams and fear reprimands for making mistakes; as a result, they are paralyzed with fear or will seek to follow the "tried and true" path of doing things. Creativity and efficiency are not their goals.

The majority of dysfunctional non-performing teams tend to consist of overworked members and lack any commitment to seeing results. Excuses, such as, "I have too much to do, then to be on another committee or team" is often uttered. The worst cases are those that tend to be superstars or lone rangers. They prefer to work alone and see the team as a hindrance to their personal success.

Finally, dysfunctional non-performing teams tend to have a high number of individuals that are suffering from burnout and mental fatigue. These may be people that have performed well previous but do to demands and constantly being asked to give more. They have a hard time saying, "No." and as a result, feel overwhelmed in their ability to contribute to the team.

Regardless of the makeup of your team, all teams will experience some level of organizing frustration which is normal in the beginning, and it's your job to help guide your team through the dynamics of team building, which Bruce Tukman identifies as:

Forming	Storming	Norming	Performing
Role uncertainty, seek outside guidance	Reject outside authority	Wanting to be part of the team	Concern with getting the job done

www.pmhut.com/the-five-stages-of-project-team-development

Build an Accountability Team

One of the best ways to keep you focused and on track is to have a team of accountability partners. I suggest a **Group Accountability Protocol**. This protocol is a set of rules for giving and receiving constructive advice. Below is a set of protocols that I use with my Power 5 Mastermind Group:

- Seek to Understand before trying to be Understood
- Get to know the person first, before criticizing their actions
- What is the intent of the criticism given?
- Are you open to listening and not respond to criticism?
- Keep the criticism constructive; it should promote healthy discussions

- Criticism should be balanced, start with what is right, and end with a positive, uplifting statement.

Aside from your accountability team, you need to team to help you be successful as well. **Please, Please, STOP** trying to do everything alone. It's not worth the frustration and only leads to burnout and anxiety. Having a team is also a powerful strategy for handling particular types of distraction. When you have a team, you can delegate.

When you delegate, you enlarge the scope of your business, increase your productivity, and in all likelihood, increase your profits. There's a skill to delegating which, if you master, will maximize everyone's efforts. The thing you must decide first is which things to delegate and which things to keep for yourself? Here are my suggestions for thing to delegate and things are best done by you.

The best things to delegate:
- Routine matters
- Responsibilities for tasks
- Low impact items (goes wrong does not significantly impact business operations)
- Tasks requiring special knowledge you don't have

Things not to delegate:

- Anything you need to do personally
- Accountability (you are accountable; they are responsible)
- Emergency tasks
- Tasks that are exceptions to the typical method of doing things
- Tasks that might have serious repercussions

What Have You Learned?

What have you learned about being a success and productive team?

_____
_____
_____
_____
_____
_____
_____
_____
_____
_____
_____
_____
_____
_____
_____
_____

Focused-Driven Lifestyle Strategies

Strategy 3: Focus on Quality

To build anything of value takes setting priorities and using your time wisely so that you can be more productive. Productivity is not about getting more done in a shorter amount of time. Productivity is about quality over quantity. I remember rushing to get the dishes done as a teen, so I could return to playing outdoors (back when kids played outdoors); only to discover that most of the dishes still had food particles on them. My mother's solution was to have me wash every dish in the house to teach me a valuable lesson. It was better to get it done right, then just to get it done. This lesson has stuck with me since then.

Chapter Five

Focus Promotes Productivity

The first thing you need to do is to start approaching your work in a more productive and efficient manner is to remove multitasking from the equation. Multi-tasking is associated with being productive, but now it has become a way of life. It's not a productive way of working. For one, it makes you inefficient for having to switch between tasks. It can complicate things, as you suffer from stress and commit errors. It can also make you insane as you deal with the chaos of multi-tasking when your brain is designed only to handle one thing.

That's why it's best to settle with a single task. Your mind will focus on one thing and one thing alone. Imagine how joyful it would be to savor one task, such as reading a novel, eating breakfast, or spending time with your family. It also feels good to lose yourself in something that you feel is worth doing.

You can lead a life full of single tasks by doing these things:

- Be aware of the things that you are doing, right from when you start doing it. Stop yourself from switching to another thing.

- Eliminate distractions. If you're going to research, focus on it alone. If you're going to read a book, do nothing except read the book.
- Choose your tasks wisely. Always ask yourself "Am I doing something worthwhile?" If not, proceed with the important tasks.
- Pour everything into the job at hand. If you're going to talk with friends, talk and listen. If you're going to lose weight, eat healthier and exercise as much as you can.
- Practice. Once you get your drive going, practice it every single day until you're good at it.

But how can you boost your productivity if you choose single tasks?

- Choose the most important tasks every day, the ones that you need to finish to create an impact on your work and life in general.
- Don't go straight to your distractions first thing in the morning.
- Instead, prepare a focus list (top 3 things to get done)
- Get rid of distractions.
- Finish your tasks one by one.
- Stop yourself when you feel the temptation to check your inbox or log into your social network accounts.
- Don't stop doing the most important tasks until completed.

- Take note of things that you can't do now or think of doing later, so you won't forget them.
- Take a break and de-stress by breathing deeply in and out.

Tim Ferriss, author of the *Four Hour Workweek* always talks about having one task that he absolutely must get completed that day and then completing that. Everything else, he considers to be 'extra.' This is generally the best attitude to take to any list of objectives. Complete the biggest and most important task first and then move onto the smaller ones.

The reason this is so important is that the biggest task is going to take the most time, the most focus and the most energy. It's also going to give you the greatest sense of satisfaction once ticked off.

If you complete all the smaller tasks first, then you risk taking up a lot of time with switching between tasks, answering emails and setting things up. This can end up taking longer than you think and then not leave enough time to complete that one 'big task' that you needed to finish. As a result, the day ends, and you're left feeling stressed.

Instead, work on that one massive task that will make a real difference first. Then start on those smaller jobs and get as many as possible out the way. You can do this after 4 pm, at the point in the day when you're starting to feel less productive.

Get into A Flow

To achieve the focused-driven lifestyle, you need to learn how to do things effortlessly. It's not always right to address your difficulties at work by giving into your distractions just to avoid dealing with the former. Instead, flow like water, effortless in its movement. It follows gravity and the contours of the landscape that it passes through. It doesn't force things, yet it's powerful and graceful. Learn how to be effortless by keeping these tips in mind: Do something out of passion. When you're about to do something you don't like change course and find something that you do like, while still getting to the same destination.

Don't force your control over uncontrollable things. Feel the moment. Keep an eye open to all the possibilities, consider them all instead of fearing all the choices, and follow your intuition. Be flexible. Find the sweet spot to maximize effectiveness and minimize effort. Do less and do them with less effort. Confront the difficult and deal with the easy things now.

Now you have just one big task to complete during your work day; you should stand a much better chance of getting into a 'flow state.' A flow state is an almost mythical state of mind that is described by many productivity gurus. The idea is that by focusing on one job that you need to complete you can eventually get into a state of mind where you're able to shut out all outside distractions and work in a fast and focused manner.

Focus on Smaller Chunks

Granted that you now know a bit about how to focus, you still have a lot of work to do. For starters, you need to narrow down your focus. It's not smart to work with a broad focus. This could be overcommitting to too many projects at once or trying to please all of your customers, doing everything for everybody. "Focus is narrowing your priorities."

Instead, you need to narrow your focus by identifying your priorities. Let go of one additional task at a time. Do less. Include fewer features. Learn to say, "no" to some people's requests. Accept that you can't please everybody. Focus on fewer things, things that matter to you, not always someone else.

Gain Better Focus at Work

To be a productive worker, you need to handle distractions well and learn the art of focusing on important things. If you're working in the service industries, the following tips might help:

- When you serve your customers, do that and that alone. Be fully present when you do your job and disregard other problems, emails, or mobile phone.
- Deal with one customer at a time.
- Try to find a chance to refocus in the middle of your work. Clear distractions or an hour or so.
- Learn to let go of some tasks on hand by automating them, delegating them, posting a FAQ section on your website, outsourcing help, or breaking your services into related sections.
- Be focused in your personal life. Learn to disconnect once you're off work and find peace of mind.

To avoid interruptions from your co-workers or staff as a boss, you might want to take note of these pointers:

- Don't make the decisions all by yourself. Let others do it too. Set parameters on when to interrupt you for decision-making.
- Schedule your unavailability. Set times when you are not to be interrupted.

- Appoint a second-in-command to help you make decisions.
- Set expectations as to when people can interrupt you when you're working.
- Focus on every problem and every interruption that comes your way.
- Focus on life outside of work and enjoy the peace and quiet while indulging in your creative hobbies and interests.

But how do you deal with your boss, if he or she is the source of your problem? Your boss might expect you to answer your calls, texts, or emails, to pull off long hours, or to work overnight. You have to deal with your boss by doing these things:

- Discuss your desire to focus on your boss. Convince him or her about how finding focus will improve your creativity and productivity.
- Determine the factors that you can control and those that you can't. Change those controllable factors to help you focus. For instance, you can better organize your desk or computer desktop. If you can't do away with ignoring emails, at least don't distract yourself by surfing the web.

- Try to work out of the office. If you have the liberty to work at home or anywhere else without distractions, do so.
- Show your boss that all these changes to find focus really work.
- Find another job. If your boss doesn't approve of your pursuit of focus, consider changing jobs.

If you do find unsupportive people around, people who do not approve of all the changes that you want to make to find focus, don't force them. Let them understand how important it is for you to be able to focus. Make sure to ask for their help. If you can't convince them with words, show them an example. Show them how the changes you planned to find focus will work. Settle with the changes that you can make, with the lack of support of other people.

Create a Focused-Driven Office Culture

Modern offices boast of being productive and efficient. However, workers are constantly interrupted by distractions, from emails and IMs to calls, calendar requests, meetings, and office chatter. All these distractions cause information overload and stress. They might even end up doing nothing at the end of the day while paying attention to a lot of distractions.

If you are an employer or supervisor, you can create a more productive environment, if you advise your employees to do these things:

- Tell them to figure out what to do for the day and settle with 3-5 important tasks. They should do this first thing in the morning.
- They should organize their desks and tune out all distractions to work on the first important task.
- They can devote about 30 minutes of your day to go to email and voicemail.
- They should focus on completing the rest of the tasks, with few interruptions.
- They should meet with you to look back on their day, discuss problems, and settle what tomorrow's tasks should be.
- They should wear headphones to drown out distractions.
- They can work at home for about two days per week, but make them report to you all the tasks that they have finished for the day.
- They should learn how to disconnect, starting with your effort to shut down the Internet for a few hours every day.

Soon enough, all these changes will accumulate to significant changes that will help you and even the people around you find focus. Just make sure to show them how it should be done.

Reduce Communication Overhead

Communication overhead is a term used to describe the negative impact that lots of meetings, emails, and phone calls can have on your productivity. When you're in a meeting, you aren't working, and when you're on the phone, you're not working! To get around this, try to keep unnecessary communication to an absolute minimum.

You can reduce this in a number of different ways. For instance, if you find yourself in lots of long phone calls, consider asking people to email instead of calling. Alternatively, preface your phone calls by telling the person you're speaking to that you only have five minutes, so you'll need to get straight to business. They may offer to call back but simply say 'no it's okay, but we'll just have to make it quick.'

As for meetings, consider discussing with your manager whether you need to be present for meetings. Try skipping one, to begin with, and explain that you have lots of work to finish and that you feel your time could be put to better use in other ways.

Take a Walk

Did you know that you can boost your productivity immensely by taking a walk during your lunch break? Aside from staying healthy and slim? You can follow this walking routine to help you regain your focus:

- Walk for about 15 to 30 minutes to a destination – a library, park, coffee shop, or café. Don't connect online.
- Work for 60 minutes, then take a short walking break. You can insert walking to get a snack or cup of tea into this routine.
- Repeat this schedule.

Walking and disconnecting are worth trying because you can refocus and can think better after sitting all day long. It will also help you clear your head, enjoy what nature has to offer and take a break from stress. It will even help you improve physically. After walking, you'll know how to focus on work again and waste less time on distractions.

Take It Slow

Living a fast-paced life seems to be everyone's game. It's common for people to multitask and switch between tasks. But doing this might be counterproductive.

If you want to create great things, you need to slow down. Rushing everything will only make more room for errors. Move slowly and accomplish the right things. Slowing down will also benefit you by being able to focus better and deeper, which will lead you to appreciate things, time, and people. When you learn to recognize this, you'll know how to enjoy life. All in all, life will be less stressful and more peaceful.

The first step towards slowing down is to change your mindset. You have to understand and get a taste of what it feels like to slow down; so you can enjoy life. Here's the key, admit to yourself how much better life gets if you learn to take it slow. To pursue life slowly, you need to do these things:

- Reduce your to-do list to essential tasks, about one to three of them (focus list). Do them first, before doing routine tasks.
- Schedule fewer meetings and focus longer amounts of time on the important things instead of being shuttled from one meeting to the next.

- Disconnect at times. Start disconnecting for short periods of time, until you can do it for a day and indulge in your creativity.
- Practice not rushing to get to appointments. Give yourself enough time to prepare for and travel to meetings instead of cramming things into your schedule.
- Know that failing to get things done is alright. You don't have to be frustrated and disappointed every time you have unfinished business.
- Eliminate, automate or delegate tasks to others.
- Be conscious of what you do, who you meet, what your surroundings look like, and more.

Don't overcommit. Choose four to five essential commitments and let go of the rest. You will feel happier and more satisfied if you don't rush everything in life.

The Pomodoro Technique

The Pomodoro Technique is another tool you can use to formalize this process. Simply use a timer and set yourself a specific amount of time that you're going to focus on your work. This can be 10 minutes, 20 minutes or 60 minutes. Work until that time is complete and the timer sounds and once that's happened, set the timer for 5 minutes to rest and relax. Then, set the timer for another block of work. Dividing your day into periods of work and rest like this helps you to maintain separation between your productivity and recovery, and this can prevent burnout while also helping you to finish more work.

Go with the Flow

The last suggestion is that no matter how much you plan your life; some things are simply out of your control. But don't get angry or disappointed because it will only stress you out and ruin your day. Instead, learn to embrace these things and go with the flow. It helps to do these things:

- Admit that you can't do everything.
- Be conscious to warrant a change.
- Take a deep breath every time you feel frustrated, angry or stressed.
- Get perspective to learn to let go of things that you can't control.
- Practice going with the flow, until you excel at it.
- Laugh it off, even if it doesn't seem funny.
- Know that you can't control other people.
- Acknowledge imperfection and change.
- See life as a powerful machine.
- Life is ever changing. Don't fight it.

What Have You Learned?

What have you learned about being productive in your life and at work?

_____
_____
_____
_____
_____
_____
_____
_____
_____
_____
_____
_____
_____
_____
_____
_____
_____
_____
_____

Chapter Six

Focus Steers Priorities

Before you can set priorities, you need to arrange things in some order. The foundation of setting priorities is organization. I can remember as a young child being at the zoo trying to look at the lions, and because they were hidden in the bushes, I was unable to see them.

Organization steers focus by allowing you to clear away the clutter that obstructs your vision. All of us go through moments of extreme clarity and focus, at other times, we need to refocus our attention so we can clearly see what is in front of us. This section explores some of the benefits of clearing away mental obstacles and physical obstacles that stand as barriers to success.

First, make a list of all the things you'd like to reorganize or change to achieve greater efficiency. It could be quite a large number of things: clearing the clutter from your desk, setting specific times to handle e-mails, beginning to clean up your inbox, etc. If you're like most people, you have a long list.

Right now, write down everything that comes to mind without thinking about what is most important versus less important. Imagine operating at your peak performance level. Then take a look at all aspects of your business or life and how you function right now. Think about all the things you need to add and all the things you need to change or discontinue to achieve your vision of peak performance. Write everything down, no matter how minor it seems.

Organize Your Home

Now you have some systems in place; you should find time to free up your day. Maybe you have a bit more energy in the evenings and are less stressed on your way to work.

The next thing is to organize your home for efficiency. This is crucial because an organized home is a reflection of an orderly mind. More than that, it can also create an orderly mind. Not only does a neat home make it easier to find things, thereby saving time and stress. You're no longer hunting for keys or trying to remember where you put that recipe or receipt the other day.

Organization makes it that much easier for you to relax at home. Our brains crave order and organization, and this is why we find things like tilted picture frames or crooked lines so distressing.

What's more, you'll have the confidence of knowing where everything is in your home, and being able to retrieve them fast. Just imagine, what it would feel like not hunting for lost items. So how do you start putting this into action? Here are some tips that will help.

Get Rid of Clutter

One of the single most important things you can do to make your home tidier; is to start throwing things out or better yet, give things away. This sounds ruthless, and at first, you might object to the idea of parting with your possessions. Reducing clutter can make your home considerably less stressful and help you to stay on top of your chores a lot more quickly.

A good place to start is with your ornaments and so-called knick-knacks. Go through all the things you have on display and throw out half of those items – or at least put them away somewhere. By doing this, you have created a much more minimal space, which is immediately going to feel less cluttered.

What's left behind will be your very favorite things. That means that those favorite items will get much more attention and focus, versus all those other things that were detracting from them. Another way to remove clutter is to find all the boxes under your bed, and in your closet, you haven't been in for the last six months. Remove anything valuable or sentimental and throw the rest out. If you haven't used it within six months, chances are, you don't need it! For documents, it's better to do what I call, scan and shred. This will reduce keeping piles of paper in boxes. I did a video on this subject which you can access by visiting YouTube: https://youtu.be/LwUPSKjHZKo.

Organizing Your Social Life

After you organize your home, look at your social life. Do ever feel like life would be a whole lot less stressful if you weren't trying to please everyone? We all feel like this from time to time – and especially when life is getting on top of us, and we don't have the time, energy or desire to devote to every friend, colleague and family members. So how do you go about organizing your social life and staying on top of all those things you need to do?

Keep a Social Calendar

If you have lots of friends and a busy social life, then this is likely to result in a lot of different things planned. One of the biggest stresses that can come from this is being double booked for multiple activities; which mean letting people down or rushing to accommodate both. Keeping a diary is an excellent way to avoid this from happening and especially if you can use an app that will let you easily update and edit events on the fly. This way you can also set up different reminders to ensure that you always know what's coming up and don't forget something big you have on your agenda.

What's even better about using an app like Google Calendar is that you can also let other people see your diary and contribute to it. This is an excellent way to arrange meetups and get-togethers because it let people see when you're free.

Now comes one of the very biggest tips for organizing your life and getting things in order: make sure that you also add your other tasks and to-do list to your diary. Ask yourself, "what are the things that I absolutely can't miss?" For instance, you might decide that you are going to go to the gym three times a week. Maybe you absolutely can't put off filling out your tax return any longer.

So make sure it's in the diary and treat it just as you would any other activity – as immutable. If someone suggests doing something on that day and you have 'fill out your tax return' already on that date, then you explain that you can't meet up, or that you'll have to get there a couple of hours later.

It seems extreme, but once you start taking your commitments seriously, you'll find you have much more time actually to do the things you want to do and that you don't feel stressed because those necessary tasks are constantly being pushed back.

Organize Your Social Calendar

If you have a busy social calendar, then it's often easy to feel overly stressed and put upon. You're constantly being asked out to events and if you say no, then you feel as though you're letting people down. We feel like we can't say "no" to a friend who invites you out because it's been a long time since you saw them.

If you're having a hard time turning down invitations, then simply remind yourself that you need to reserve the lion's share of your time and energy for your family. This doesn't make you a bad person; it makes you an adult with responsibilities! This doesn't mean that you're going to cut off contact with your friends or tell them you don't want to see them anymore! All it means is that you might – for example – only accept one invitation to spend time with friends a week. Or more realistically, two a month as you start to get older.

Score Your Friendships

That means that if you have two invitations from two sets of friends, you might simply decide which friend is one that adds the most value to you. You can assign a number system based on how you feel when you are with certain people. For example, a score of 5 would be someone that you could spend hours with and not feel drained. Instead, you felt empowered and energized being in their presence. On the other hand, a score of 1 would be someone who completely drains your energy, and you can tolerate for a limited amount of time, say 45 minutes.

This scoring system is not exclusively referring to friends, but rather all the contacts you maintain whether they be friends, colleagues, associates or acquaintances. In reality, you can probably only maintain about seven close relationships – so choose carefully who those seven are going to be!

Fire Your Frenemies

One thing that makes this a lot easier is to think about all the friends you have that aren't friends. These are the people who we count as friends but who we don't enjoy spending time around all that much. These are the friends who we always moan about to our other friends. And these are the friends who let us down.

As you get older, and the stakes get higher, you need to eliminate those who are not your real friends. As such, it's time to put those people to one side and to focus on the ones who you enjoy spending time with, and who are there for you. Just as removing some of the unnecessary items from your life can help to put more emphasis on your favorite belongings; you likewise enjoy closer relationships with people who matter to you. In other words, spend less or no time with people who don't deserve your time and energy.

Organize Your Time

The first and absolute most important point to consider when organizing your time is that you must recognize your limitations. This is where a lot of us go wrong because we forget that our energy is finite as well as our time. A perfect example of getting this wrong is if you write yourself a new training program and diet. You plan to lose weight by working out three additional hours on top of your routine while also dieting.

So you now have less energy, and you're expected to start exerting yourself for a total of three hours, as well as traveling to and from the gym? This just doesn't work. If you find that you currently aren't doing all the things you would like to be doing, then once again you need to organize your time.

Value Your Time

Successful entrepreneurs aren't 'yes' men or women. These are people who value their time and who want to invest that time wisely. Whether you're an entrepreneur or not, try to take the same approach. Your time is the most valuable asset you have, and eventually, it will run out.

Don't waste it working on projects you don't care about, spending time with people you don't like. Guard your time fiercely and use it in ways that're conducive to helping you get what YOU want. This is why it's important to prune your social calendar and to learn to say 'no' more often.

But it should also change the way you think about your time. Every decision you make ultimately comes down to what the best way to utilize your time is. When you get a text from a friend at work, you have to decide whether it's worth answering or continue getting work done.

Most of us trade our time for money in our careers. When you think about this and when you think about how little time you have to do the things you love, then hopefully this will motivate you to go out there and chase what your worth.

And hopefully, it will make you realize that you should fight for all the free time you have around your work – whether that means your commute, or just trying to organize flex-time or the chance to work from home.

Log Your Time

Throughout this book, I have encouraged you to write things down and to keep a record as for how you spend your time. For those of you who prefer to use software, I recommend that you visit my website at www.lifewithafocus.com/products.

I personally use a tool call Goals on Track to track my goals and tasks. I encourage you to get my book on journaling entitled, *7 Minute Day Lifestyle Journal* which can also be purchased on my website or at Amazon.com.

Identifying Your Time Sappers

Have you ever spent an entire day busily at your computer and felt like you achieved nothing at the end of it? If so, you have company!

By now you should have kept a time log of exactly how you spent your time each day, preferably for a week, so you have lots of data to work with. The next step is to analyze the data to discover exactly which time sappers are interfering with your productivity.

Time sappers are all the distractions and interruptions of any kind that take you away from working on your priority tasks and projects. Studies have shown that the things that kill your efficiency fall into four areas:

- Lack of planning
- Lack of organization
- Lack of self-management
- Lack of managing the work environment

LACK OF PLANNING
- No written goals
- Indecisiveness
- Unrealistic time estimates
- Inefficient use of waiting time
- Too much work for time allotted
- Poor decisions
- Failure to break down tasks completely
- Not enough review at steps during process

DISORGANIZATION
- General disorganization (messy desk, unworkable filing)
- Procrastination

- Unfinished tasks

LACK OF SELF-MANAGEMENT
- Taking on too much
- Not enough delegation
- Not saying "no."
- Perfectionism
- Media surfing
- Poor self-discipline
- Faulty listening and note taking
- Absenteeism or lateness

LACK OF MANAGING THE WORK ENVIRONMENT
- Drop-in visitors
- Media and phone interruptions
- Unnecessary paperwork
- Unnecessary meetings
- Confusing directions

Use this list to decide which time sappers show up in your day.

Some will probably be easier to get rid of than others. Some may have become habits that are hard to break. But make a start. For instance, if your weaknesses are surfing the internet, cut down the amount of time you spend doing that per day or only do it at a set time during the day.

It may be easier for you to eliminate these time sappers a few at a time or one at a time, but write down a date when you will
address each one and then do it. Review your list from time to time to see that you're making progress. Making these changes will be worth it when you see the increase in your productivity.

Recovery Time

In the Netflix series, Super Girl, a.k.a. Kara who is a Kryptonian refugee who begins to embrace her super powers and becomes the hero of her city, like her cousin Clark Kent. In one episode, she fights her main antagonist uncle Nun who vowed to make Earth like the Kryptonians' destroyed their home planet, Krypton. After battling her uncle Nun, she discovers she has lost her powers and needed a few days to recover.

Likewise, you need to give yourself time to recover. We are much more productive overall when we have been given some time to recover and to recharge our batteries. If you are just constantly doing one thing after another, then eventually you'll become tired, and you'll stop working properly.

When to schedule recovery time, it's useful to consider the natural ebbs and flows of your energy. All of us have times of day where we are more productive and times of day where we crash. Most of us, for instance, will find we crash when getting in from work and that we're less productive at work after 4 pm.

Also important to take into account is the way our other activities impact on our energy levels. One of the easiest ways to make yourself exhausted is to eat dinner! Once you've eaten, your body needs time and energy to digest food, and that leaves you with little energy to do anything else.

So instead of making dinner, eating on the sofa and then planning on cleaning, you should complete the cleaning before eating. Don't sit on the couch if you want to keep your energy levels up. You can always enjoy a light snack when you get in from work if you're too hungry to do anything else!

A Few More Tips on Being Organized

Below are twenty tips to keep you organized:

- ✓ Keep Everything in Its Place - Sounds simple but practicing it takes will power and consistency so you can form a habit.

- ✓ Keep a Focus List – Record your three most important tasks and focus on them until they are finished.
- ✓ Simplify your surroundings – get rid of clutter!
- ✓ Put things away when you are done using them! Why wait and clutter your work area?
- ✓ Figure out what time of day you are at your personal peak - schedule important tasks for that time.
- ✓ For a more productive day - simply get up earlier.
- ✓ Set deadlines for your own personal tasks and strive to meet them.
- ✓ Don't be afraid to take control of your time. Focus on
- ✓ the tasks that YOU need to complete.
- ✓ Keep your working area tidy.
- ✓ Find office or household items that have more than one use - unless required, avoid specialty tools that
- ✓ only have one single use.
- ✓ Be decisive! Don't over think things - make a clear cut decision and follow it.
- ✓ Always plan your tasks ahead. A little planning at the start will save a lot of time in the long run.
- ✓ Batch up your tasks. It can be more efficient to do similar tasks all at once. Try keeping all of your phone call messages for a certain period (30 days) for example.

- ✓ Commit to changing problem behaviors. If you are honest with yourself, you will be able to pinpoint daily activities that keep you from being organized.
- ✓ Make the time. If you are a busy person, then schedule some organizing time right into your daily calendar.
- ✓ Outsource. If there is a task that you hate doing (even organization itself), then outsource it to a company that specializes in it.
- ✓ Don't forget the ultimate organization tool - the trash can. Throw out anything you don't need, and you will never have to "organize" it.
- ✓ For efficiency, purposes work in time "power blocks." Focus and work hard on a task for 60-90 minutes and then break for 5 (or a similar type time split).
- ✓ Just start. Start getting organized and developing habits that will improve your efficiency. It can be a struggle, but persistence and a positive attitude will help you persevere.

The next step is prioritizing your changes. This is an individual thing. You could start with things you believe most urgently need changing, or you could start with some things that are relatively easy to do, just to get you started and to get them out of the way. Again, write down everything you want to change, organize better, or become more efficient. Be very specific. Break down the tasks into the smallest pieces possible.

Your Daily Action Plan should be in front of you at all times. It's your primary tool for staying on track to accomplish your goals. Even though it takes a little time for you to complete it, it has benefits for you right from the start. It will help you:

- Reduce stress because since you planned your day already, you'll be working at top efficiency.
- Improve productivity since your priorities are clear from the beginning of the day.
- Make clear progress toward your goals since your actions are mapped out for you.
- Help you achieve a balance between all parts of your life since you scheduled work time, and you have unscheduled time for the other areas of your life.

For many people, it's hard to find focus because there are too many things that they are trying to accomplish all at once. That's why you need to learn to prioritize things. Start with reducing your tasks. Choose the five most important tasks in your to-do list and deal with them first. Devote a block of your day to doing the rest of the routine tasks.

Among essential tasks, start with the one that excites you the most and the one that will have the biggest impact on your life. Settle with a single task at a time. Start working on it for 45 minutes. Take a 5-minute break, then focus on it for 60 minutes or longer, until you get the momentum of things.

TURBO Charging your Priorities

You can prioritize based on various criteria:

- **Importance** – the important items are the ones that will bring you the biggest payoff.
- **Urgency** – these items will have the most severe results if you don't get them done.
- **Quickest benefit** – these will bring results for you very soon.
- **Most difficult** – this is the most difficult item on your list, and you want to do it first to get it out of the way.
- **First domino effect** – this item needs to be done. First, you can't change other things until you change it.
- **Desire** – these are the items you most want to change.

To go even farther and to TURBO charge your priorities, follow this simple format:

Time Stamp your projects. Get in the habit of setting a deadline for everything you do. When you have a conversation with someone, and there is an expectation of receiving or obtaining information; it is crucial that a timetable is established for when you will follow-up with your clients, colleagues or friends.

Understand the purpose of the project. When you understand the reason or purpose for engaging your energy into a project, it's easier to stay focus and committed to its completion. Before agreeing to do anything of significance find out the purpose and intent for doing it. For example, I get asked to attend a lot of product pitches, and all of them promise to be the next big thing. When presented with these money-making opportunities, I will ask myself, "what would be the purpose of me attending? Does this fit into my overall focus?

Resources required. Another question to ask yourself, "Do I have the resources (time, skills, finances) to commit to this project? It has been my experience that most people fail to succeed in accomplishing their goals in life due to a lack of needed resources, or they depleted their resources; so the project stalls or dies incomplete.

Bundle into a project. Sometimes the task is too big or requires several steps to get done. In the same way, telecommunication companies combine or bundle your mobile, cable TV, and internet service; you should take the same approach and combine similar tasks together. For example, when I write a paper, I will take one day to do the research, the second day to organize and write an outline, the third day is writing the draft with the fourth-day editing, and the fifth day I will submit the paper. By breaking the assignment into small chunks, I don't feel overwhelmed with anxiety.

Outcome metrics. The final step used to **TURBO** charge your priorities has a way to measure your success by asking this question, "How will I track and measure the results of the project? A simple measure would be to create a score card as the example below indicates:

Date Started	Date End	Results	Notes
September 6	September 12	1	ahead of schedule

Note: Results (Yes = 1, No = 0)

What Have You Learned?
Write down your key priorities:

_____

Strategy 4: Adjust Your Focus

A major aspect of developing your focus is having the ability to adjust. Just like the lens of a camera, there are times when you have to make an adjustment to bring the camera into focus. In order to train your mind to do this, simply sit in a quiet room and focus on one thing, when other thoughts enter your mind, don't ignore them, simply write them down, and refocus. Once you do this exercise a few times, you will condition your brain to concentrate on one thing at a time it will automatically discard other thoughts. It's about learning to tune out the noise so you can hear the lyrics. Another exercise is to walk into a room where several conversations are going on, focus on one conversation, this will help you to focus as well.

Chapter Seven

Refocus Your Focus

Five days a week, I have the pleasure of participating in a mastermind group that I started along with my friend Brian Keith Jenkins. Every day, I end with the following statement, *Get Focused, Refocus so that you can Live a life with a Focus.* Like a camera lens has to be adjusted, your focus also has to be refocused or adjusted at times. So how do you adjust your focus? A good place to start is with your vision and how you mentally picture what you want your life to look like ideally.

What you might also find, is that once you start visualizing the lifestyle you want, it might impact what your life will look like in the future. For example, you might think you want to get rich – but if your vision is mostly about living in a beautiful home, or traveling a lot, then maybe the money is just a means to an end? Maybe your real vision or focus is to have a better home, or to travel more? And maybe there are better ways to accomplish those things! Another favorite tip is to imagine writing your eulogy.

The point is to imagine that you have died, and you're writing the speech you would like to be given at your funeral. In other words, how do you want to be remembered? Do you talk about what a family man you were? Or about how you had a life filled with adventures?

Refocus Your Daily Habits

Second, after you have refocused your vision, you should look at your daily habits. For example, if you're one of those people who have an extremely difficult time with breaking old habits, here are some tips that might work for you:

- ✓ **Break one habit at a time**. If change is very difficult for you, focus on just one change at a time. Replace an old habit with a new one, one habit at a time and stick with that one change until you feel comfortable that you won't go back to your old habit. Habits are not easy to break, and some are much harder than others. You might disagree, but think about how often you tweet or check your Facebook page. That probably makes the point very clear to some of you. (Ha ha.)

- ✓ **Small habits.** Here's another tip for making changes in a gentler way. I only need to remind you of New Year's resolutions here. You probably know that gym memberships are at their peak at New Year's and that most people never use those memberships. The people who do use them drop off after the first month. For a lot of people, it's just too much of a change. They have to give up their free time, get themselves to the gym, and then actually exercise. It all seems like a good idea, but then reality sets in. It's much better to start by trying to change a smaller habit – for instance, cut your coffee drinking from 6 cups to 2 cups a day. You might have more success with that than trying to cut out coffee completely. The point is that if you have 20 things you'd like to change and change is difficult for you, start with one small thing. This will give you the confidence to go on to bigger items.

- ✓ **Focus on starting**. For instance, if you're very out of shape and haven't exercised for a while, don't set your goal at running a marathon. Maybe it's a good long-term goal, but in the short term, walking or running around the block is something you might be able to do without getting so discouraged that you'll quit. Just get started. So many people fail, not because they don't have big dreams and good intentions, but because they just can't get started. Many times if people just start something, they realize it's not as hard as they thought.

- ✓ **Don't miss two straight days.** Get back on the horse. For instance, you don't enjoy filling out your action plan and you not sure it's worth the trouble, so you skip a day. That's really not being fair yourself. If you haven't seen progress in your organization and efficiency, it's very likely because you haven't been at it long enough. Getting off-track for one day and getting back on track is a lot better than quitting. Don't quit.

Refocus with New Hobbies

Another way to refocus is by starting a new hobby that does not involve the use of a computer, tablet, or smartphone. Just think, many of our hobbies involve a screen of some sort —whether it's gaming, watching films or using the computer. There's nothing wrong with this per say, but it sure can stress you out over time and lead to burn out if it's all you're doing to relax.

To avoid this situation, make sure that you have some hobbies in your life that don't involve screens, and that require sustained focus and attention. A good example of that would be reading. Reading a book not only offers a reprieve from the screen but it also means that you need to stay focused on that one thing for a good amount of time.

Instead of moving from one information stream to the next, your mind is completely focused and relaxed. This is almost like meditation.

Going to the gym or playing sports is also good and so are things like DIY, walking… anything where your phone stays in your pocket. And then make sure that you abide by this rule and keep your phone away for this duration. Again, if you're anxious about missing something important then consider using a smartwatch. Or perhaps just setting ringtones for priority callers.

Focused Meditation

Perhaps the most meditative hobby you can take up though is… meditation! Meditation is simply the act of taking control of your inner monolog and using it to bring your mind to calm.

Different forms of meditation work differently–mindfulness vs. transcendental for instance – but they both offer the same benefits. Not only is meditation shown to be superb for us in the short-term by helping to encourage slower brain waves, but it also provides tools for combating stress and staying focused as necessary.

Have Quiet Time

The point at which your phones and computers become most detracting is in the evening. Not only do screens stress us out but the light itself also causes the release of cortisol – which acts against the release of melatonin. In other words, our brain treats a phone screen just like natural sunlight and prevents us from getting into a dormant state of mind.

There are many solutions to this – some of which get quite ridiculous and include things like wearing blue-blocking shades to bed. Though, the most efficient way avoid light from screens before bed is simply to stop using computers and phones for at least an hour before you go to sleep. Let your friends know that you'll be doing this, or even consider setting up and auto text response that is triggered after this time (Android apps like Tasker can help you do this).

And better yet, use half an hour to read a book or something before you doze off. This will quiet your mind and help you to get deeper sleep once you do hit the hay. And it goes without saying that when you get home at the end of the day and are off work, you do not answer any emails that are related to work. Don't even look at your work email – it will only prevent you from properly relaxing and enjoying your time off!

More Lifestyle Tips

We've already addressed the value of meditation, and this is a great tool you can use to keep your mind relaxed. If you find that you struggle a lot with stress, then you should also think about addressing the sources of that stress, which may even mean quitting your job. You can also try seeing a therapist. Often the most efficient form of therapy for stress is 'CBT' (cognitive behavioral therapy) which will help to teach you the mental tools and skills that can help you to eliminate unhelpful thoughts and anxieties.

Finally, if you can find the time and the energy, it is very much worth spending some time on a basic exercise regime. Even if your goal isn't to lose weight or build muscle, exercising will directly help to give you more energy and focus throughout the day. It acts as a natural depressant, improves the energy efficiency of your cells and even helps you to get more energy to your brain. AND it leads to better sleep!

What Have You Learned?

Write down what you have learned about refocusing your focus?

_____
_____
_____

Focused-Driven Lifestyle Strategies

Strategy 5: Ask for Help

When you think of successful people like Oprah Winfrey, Steve Jobs of Apple, and Bill Gates, it important to know that while we are aware of their names and accomplishments, what is less known are the people who help them become successful. As an example, when Oprah Winfrey retired after twenty-five years and set out to create the OWN (Oprah Winfrey Network).

She made several huge mistakes; the biggest was thinking that everyone who watched her on network television would automatically follow her, she was mistaken. Second, she did not have great programming in the early years. It was too much like other cable shows; her loyal fans wanted more empowerment television. Another mistake was trying to start a network while doing The Oprah Winfrey Show. As Oprah noted, *"One jockey can't ride two horses at the same time and win."*

Then she sought the help of her friend, Tyler Perry who was able to produce several groundbreakings shows cheaper than anyone else and soon her ratings and viewership rose. She learned that while she was hugely successful on network television, it was a different game being on cable television. She had realized before it was too late that she needed help. One lesson learned by Oprah, *"it's not ever wise to initiate customer facing operations without 100 percent leadership attention and focus" (entrepreneur.com/article/224189).*

Chapter Eight

Focus Drives Humility

Several years ago, my good friend Mark Anthony Garrett (www.teachersareheros.com) gave me some great advice about working on multiple projects. He said, "Lyman focus on what you do best, and simply outsource the rest." His advice allowed me to build a successful business and accomplish many of my goals. When you are focused, you understand that you can't and should not try to be Super Man or Super Woman. These heroes also need help at times.

In this chapter, I will discuss how focus drives humility. Humility can be defined as the *quality or state of not thinking you are better than other people* (www.merriam-webster.com).

In essence, humility allows you to seek help from others. Outsourcing has been one of the most important factors of my business model. Since outsourcing some tasks, I have been able to promote a spirit of excellence throughout my business and also in my personal life as well. Too often we try to do everything ourselves which is counterproductive to focus.

When you outsource things to someone who with the skills and expertise; frees you from being mediocre and direct your energies towards the things you are great at doing.

This also applies to the way you're spending money. If spending money means you can buy back more time, then this will very often be an excellent use of your money. That might mean outsourcing work such as cleaning to a cleaner, or it might mean getting a dishwasher. There are many other ways you can outsource your tasks and get more time back.

For example, consider hiring a 'virtual assistant.' These are people who will complete any task for you that can be completed remotely. In other words, the service operates only by email and over the phone, which means that they can handle things for you like making appointments, arranging meetings, doing research and answering emails.

Traditionally, virtual assistants are used by entrepreneurs and small businesses. However, they can also be used for a range of personal tasks whether that means booking a table at a restaurant, researching your next car or suggesting holidays!

The best bit about virtual assistants is that they tend to be incredibly affordable: often they will charge as little as $3 for an hour of work. The limitation, other than the fact that they must work remotely, is that you will be outsourcing to India. There are many other ways to outsource your work too. Just understand that this can be a great way to invest your money and think of it as buying time.

Focus Drives Humility

Perhaps, one of the greatest lessons I had to learn after graduating from college was that I needed help. I thought, my college education would prepare me for the real world. Let me say; I was only partly correct. College gave me a great foundation. However, actual work experience provided me with the structure and skills I needed to be successful. In other words, I needed to humble myself and shed my ego to ask for help.

Once I realized that I needed help, my career as a recruiter blossom. I can recall asking a senior recruiter, Gary how he was able to meet his recruitment goals and still have time to leave the office on time, while I was spending 13 hours a day in the office and barely met my recruitment targets. Gary's explanation. He said, *"Lyman, I don't try to do everything alone, I use my network, and if you want to be successful in this business, I suggest you build a network."* Then, he offered to help me. My ego wanted to say, *"no thank you,* but my heart said, *"Gary, I would appreciate that very much."*

Why Ask Friends for Help?

Another way that focus drives humility is when you ask your friends for help. The reality is that friends are there to help each other, and this cuts both ways. If you are struggling with a large number of tasks and feeling overwhelmed, chances are your friends will want to help you.

I have three very close friends that I trust to give me a dose of reality when I need it and to bounce ideas off; especially when stuck working on a project. One of my friends, Janet More (https://geekappealacademy.com/mentoring) is very good at this; she has a keen sense of what works and what doesn't work when it comes to visual aesthetics. To be honest, there are times I disagree with Janet, but 99.9% of the time after reflecting on what she said, I will agree with her assessment. She has saved me hundreds, if not thousands of dollars with her wisdom and advice.

There are many other examples, such as moving to another home or office. Instead of spending all your time and energy moving things yourself, consider asking a friend if they'll help you organize your possessions and transport them to your new home. Meanwhile, if you find you don't have time to look for holiday ideas, why not just ask your friends if they have any good recommendations?

And if you're struggling, and you don't have time to pick up your children from school, then why not ask another parent if they can help? Often you can share the burden with friends as a way to reduce your workload too. Why not take turns picking up your kids from school? That way you'll have to spend almost 50% less time driving to and from the school! Likewise, you could even agree to a similar system for your weekly shopping.

Of course, you don't want to take advantage of your friends and keep getting them to do things for you. But when you're struggling, there is nothing wrong with just asking for a little help; you'd do the same for them! And when it's mutually beneficial, then there's no downside!

Sometimes you might find yourself doing too much for your friends or shouldering too much of the work and chores at home. In either of these situations, being focused is also being able to say "No!" This means speaking up and telling your friends, family or partner that you're going to have to start doing a little less. If you keep getting more and more work piled on you, it will become profoundly disheartening – and feel like you're carrying other people.

Ask Your Employer for Help

Often, the culprit is your boss or co-worker. Don't be afraid to speak up and tell your employer or coworkers that you have too much work on your plate and that you need help. Asking your employer for help is not a sign of weakness, it shows that you are human and care about the quality of work, not just the quantity of work done. Here are several tactics you can use to ask for help:

- "I have several projects I'm working on currently; which one should I give priority?"
- "I would love to help. However, I don't have time to work on this and get my other work done. Is there someone else who can help?"
- "I'm sorry, I don't feel that I have the experience or skills to do a great job on this, I know you care about quality, so I don't think I would add any value."
- "I can get to this, when do you need it by? As you know, I'm currently working on...."
- "You may have forgotten that I'm currently already overbooked, who else can I get to assist with this?
- "Is there a way this can be divided up among the team? I'm willing to do a portion of the work, but I don't have the time to take on the whole project."

This all comes back to valuing your time!

Another tactic is asking for additional compensation; especially when the work is outside of your regular duties. You will be surprised what you can get your employer to agree to by simply asking for help, whether it be physical assistance or an increase in pay.

What Have You Learned?

Write down three lessons you have learned from this chapter.

_____
_____
_____
_____
_____
_____
_____
_____
_____
_____
_____
_____
_____
_____
_____
_____

Strategy 6: Focus on Consistency

Consistency is about your repeated actions. In reality, everyone is consistent. For example, the person who breaks his word repeatedly is consistent in not honoring his obligations. Being consistent is about making daily habits without consciously thinking about doing them. Once you have developed the ability to be consistent in doing the things that promote your success, they will become as if they were on autopilot.

A clear example of this is changing your eating habits. At first, it may be tempting to eat unhealthy foods, such as fast foods, but once you discipline your mind and start eating healthy, your desire for the unhealthy foods will begin to fade. I stopped eating fast foods, and it was tempting at first driving past the golden arches; however, within two months the temptation was gone.

Chapter Nine

Take the 30 Day Get Focused Challenge
Day 1

Morning Exercise: Sit on the side of your bed, close your eyes, take three deep breaths (through your nose) and exhale slowly through your mouth, afterwards say, "I am Focused", repeat 2 x and sit quietly for 30 seconds focusing only on your breathing, nothing else. After 30 seconds (use alarm on your phone or clock), write down what you were feeling and if you were able to only focus on your breathing and nothing else.

_____
_____
_____
_____
_____
_____

Evening Exercise: Before going to bed, while sitting, take three deep breaths (through your nose) and exhale slowly

Focused-Driven Lifestyle Strategies

through your mouth, afterwards say, "I'm grateful I retained my Focus for the day, repeat 2 x and sit quietly for 30 seconds focusing on one task that you will get done the following day, nothing else. After 30 seconds (use alarm on your phone or clock), write down what you were feeling and if you were able to focus on one task you will complete the following day and nothing else. This should take a total of 7 minutes to complete: 1 minute doing the task, 3 minutes to plan your next day (one task to get done), and 3 minutes to write your feelings about completing today's Challenge in your journal.

_____

_____

_____

_____

_____

_____

_____

Day 2

Morning Exercise: Sit on the side of your bed, close your eyes, take three deep breaths (through your nose) and exhale slowly through your mouth, afterwards say, "I am Focused", repeat 2 x and sit quietly for 30 seconds focusing only on your breathing, nothing else. After 30 seconds (use alarm on your phone or clock), write down what you were feeling and if you were able to only focus on your breathing and nothing else.

_____
_____
_____
_____
_____
_____
_____
_____

Evening Exercise: Before going to bed, while sitting, take three deep breaths (through your nose) and exhale slowly through your mouth, afterwards say, "I'm grateful I retained my Focus for the day, repeat 2 x and sit quietly for 30 seconds focusing on one task that you will get done the following day, nothing else. After 30 seconds (use alarm on your phone or clock), write down what you were feeling and if you were able to focus on one task you will complete the following day and nothing else. This should take a total of 7 minutes to complete: 1 minute doing the task, 3 minutes to plan your next day (one task to get done), and 3 minutes to write your feelings about completing today's Challenge in your journal.

_____
_____
_____
_____
_____
_____

Day 3

Morning Exercise: Sit on the side of your bed, close your eyes, take three deep breaths (through your nose) and exhale slowly through your mouth, afterwards say, "I am Focused", repeat 2 x and sit quietly for 30 seconds focusing only on your breathing, nothing else. After 30 seconds (use alarm on your phone or clock), write down what you were feeling and if you were able to only focus on your breathing and nothing else.

_____
_____
_____
_____
_____
_____

Evening Exercise: Before going to bed, while sitting, take three deep breaths (through your nose) and exhale slowly through your mouth, afterwards say, "I'm grateful I retained my Focus for the day, repeat 2 x and sit quietly for 30 seconds focusing on one task that you will get done the following day, nothing else. After 30 seconds (use alarm on your phone or clock), write down what you were feeling and if you were able to focus on one task you will complete the following day and nothing else. This should take a total of 7 minutes to complete: 1 minute doing the task, 3 minutes to plan your next day (one task to get done), and 3 minutes to write your feelings about completing today's Challenge in your journal.

_____
_____
_____
_____
_____
_____

Day 4

Morning Exercise: Sit on the side of your bed, close your eyes, take three deep breaths (through your nose) and exhale slowly through your mouth, afterwards say, "I am Focused", repeat 2 x and sit quietly for 30 seconds focusing only on your breathing, nothing else. After 30 seconds (use alarm on your phone or clock), write down what you were feeling and if you were able to only focus on your breathing and nothing else.

Focused-Driven Lifestyle Strategies

_____
_____
_____
_____
_____
_____

Evening Exercise: Before going to bed, while sitting, take three deep breaths (through your nose) and exhale slowly through your mouth, afterwards say, "I'm grateful I retained my Focus for the day, repeat 2 x and sit quietly for 30 seconds focusing on one task that you will get done the following day, nothing else. After 30 seconds (use alarm on your phone or clock), write down what you were feeling and if you were able to focus on one task you will complete the following day and nothing else. This should take a total of 7 minutes to complete: 1 minute doing the task, 3 minutes to plan your next day (one task to get done), and 3 minutes to write your feelings about completing today's Challenge in your journal.

_____
_____
_____
_____
_____

Day 5

Morning Exercise: Sit on side of your bed, close your eyes, take three deep breaths (through your nose) and exhale slowly through your mouth, afterwards say, "I am Focused", repeat 2 x and sit quietly for 30 seconds focusing only on your breathing, nothing else. After 30 seconds (use alarm on your phone or clock), write down what you were feeling and if you were able to only focus on your breathing and nothing else.

_____
_____
_____
_____
_____
_____
_____

Evening Exercise: Before going to bed, while sitting, take three deep breaths (through your nose) and exhale slowly through your mouth, afterwards say, "I'm grateful I retained my Focus for the day, repeat 2 x and sit quietly for 30 seconds focusing on one task that you will get done the following day, nothing else. After 30 seconds (use alarm on your phone or clock), write down what you were feeling and if you were able to focus on one task you will complete the following day and nothing else. This should take a total of 7 minutes to complete: 1 minute doing the task, 3 minutes to plan your next day (one task to get done), and 3 minutes to write your feelings about completing today's Challenge in your journal.

_____
_____
_____
_____
_____
_____

Day 6

Morning Exercise: Sit on side of your bed, close your eyes, take three deep breaths (through your nose) and exhale slowly through your mouth, afterwards say, "I am Focused", repeat 2 x and sit quietly for 30 seconds focusing only on your breathing, nothing else. After 30 seconds (use alarm on your phone or clock), write down what you were feeling and if you were able to only focus on your breathing and nothing else.

_____
_____
_____
_____
_____
_____
_____

Evening Exercise: Before going to bed, while sitting, take three deep breaths (through your nose) and exhale slowly through your mouth, afterwards say, "I'm grateful I retained my Focus for the day, repeat 2 x and sit quietly for 30 seconds focusing on one task that you will get done the following day, nothing else. After 30 seconds (use alarm on your phone or clock), write down what you were feeling and if you were able to focus on one task you will complete the following day and nothing else. This should take a total of 7 minutes to complete: 1 minute doing the task, 3 minutes to plan your next day (one task to get done), and 3 minutes to write your feelings about completing today's Challenge in your journal.

_____
_____
_____
_____
_____
_____

Day 7

Morning Exercise: Sit on side of your bed, close your eyes, take three deep breaths (through your nose) and exhale slowly through your mouth, afterwards say, "I am Focused", repeat 2 x and sit quietly for 30 seconds focusing only on your breathing, nothing else. After 30 seconds (use alarm on your phone or clock), write down what you were feeling and if you were able to only focus on your breathing and nothing else.

_____
_____
_____
_____
_____

Evening Exercise: Before going to bed, while sitting, take three deep breaths (through your nose) and exhale slowly through your mouth, afterwards say, "I'm grateful I retained my Focus for the day, repeat 2 x and sit quietly for 30 seconds focusing on one task that you will get done the following day, nothing else. After 30 seconds (use alarm on your phone or clock), write down what you were feeling and if you were able to focus on one task you will complete the following day and nothing else. This should take a total of 7 minutes to complete: 1 minute doing the task, 3 minutes to plan your next day (one task to get done), and 3 minutes to write your feelings about completing today's Challenge in your journal.

_____
_____
_____
_____

Day 8

Morning Exercise: First thing in the morning, sit on side of your bed, close your eyes, take three deep breaths (through your nose) and exhale slowly through your mouth, afterwards say, "I am Focused", repeat 2 x and place a pencil directly in front of you and for 30 seconds focus on nothing but the pencil. After 30 seconds (use alarm on your phone or clock), write down what you were feeling and if you were able to only focus on the pencil and nothing else. This should take a total of 2 minutes to complete.

_____
_____
_____
_____
_____

Evening Exercise: Before going to bed, while sitting, take three deep breaths (through your nose) and exhale slowly through your mouth, afterwards say, "I'm grateful I retained my Focus for the day", repeat 2 x and sit quietly for 30 seconds focusing on two tasks that you will get done the following day, nothing else. This should take a total of 7 minutes to complete: 1 minute doing the task, 3 minutes to plan your next day (one task to get done), and 3 minutes to write your feelings about completing today's Challenge in your journal.

_____
_____
_____
_____
_____
_____
_____
_____
_____
_____
_____
_____

Day 9

Morning Exercise: First thing in the morning, sit on side of your bed, close your eyes, take three deep breaths (through your nose) and exhale slowly through your mouth, afterwards say, "I am Focused", repeat 2 x and place a pencil directly in front of you and for 30 seconds focus on nothing but the pencil. After 30 seconds (use alarm on your phone or clock), write down what you were feeling and if you were able to only focus on the pencil and nothing else. This should take a total of 2 minutes to complete.

_____
_____
_____
_____
_____
_____

Evening Exercise: Before going to bed, while sitting, take three deep breaths (through your nose) and exhale slowly through your mouth, afterwards say, "I'm grateful I retained my Focus for the day", repeat 2 x and sit quietly for 30 seconds focusing on two tasks that you will get done the following day, nothing else. This should take a total of 7 minutes to complete: 1 minute doing the task, 3 minutes to plan your next day (one task to get done), and 3 minutes to write your feelings about completing today's Challenge in your journal.

_____
_____
_____
_____
_____
_____

Day 10

Morning Exercise: First thing in the morning, sit on side of your bed, close your eyes, take three deep breaths (through your nose) and exhale slowly through your mouth, afterwards say, "I am Focused", repeat 2 x and place a pencil directly in front of you and for 30 seconds focus on nothing but the pencil. After 30 seconds (use alarm on your phone or clock), write down what you were feeling and if you were able to only focus on the pencil and nothing else. This should take a total of 2 minutes to complete.

_____
_____
_____
_____
_____
_____

Evening Exercise: Before going to bed, while sitting, take three deep breaths (through your nose) and exhale slowly through your mouth, afterwards say, "I'm grateful I retained my Focus for the day", repeat 2 x and sit quietly for 30 seconds focusing on two tasks that you will get done the following day, nothing else. This should take a total of 7 minutes to complete: 1 minute doing the task, 3 minutes to plan your next day (one task to get done), and 3 minutes to write your feelings about completing today's Challenge in your journal.

_____
_____
_____
_____
_____
_____

Day 11

Morning Exercise: First thing in the morning, sit on side of your bed, close your eyes, take three deep breaths (through your nose) and exhale slowly through your mouth, afterwards say, "I am Focused", repeat 2 x and place a pencil directly in front of you and for 30 seconds focus on nothing but the pencil. After 30 seconds (use alarm on your phone or clock), write down what you were feeling and if you were able to only focus on the pencil and nothing else. This should take a total of 2 minutes to complete.

_____
_____
_____
_____
_____
_____

Evening Exercise: Before going to bed, while sitting, take three deep breaths (through your nose) and exhale slowly through your mouth, afterwards say, "I'm grateful I retained my Focus for the day", repeat 2 x and sit quietly for 30 seconds focusing on two tasks that you will get done the following day, nothing else. This should take a total of 7 minutes to complete: 1 minute doing the task, 3 minutes to plan your next day (one task to get done), and 3 minutes to write your feelings about completing today's Challenge in your journal.

_____
_____
_____
_____
_____
_____
_____
_____
_____
_____

Day 12

Morning Exercise: First thing in the morning, sit on side of your bed, close your eyes, take three deep breaths (through your nose) and exhale slowly through your mouth, afterwards say, "I am Focused", repeat 2 x and place a pencil directly in front of you and for 30 seconds focus on nothing but the pencil. After 30 seconds (use alarm on your phone or clock), write down what you were feeling and if you were able to only focus on the pencil and nothing else. This should take a total of 2 minutes to complete.

_____
_____
_____
_____
_____
_____
_____

Evening Exercise: Before going to bed, while sitting, take three deep breaths (through your nose) and exhale slowly through your mouth, afterwards say, "I'm grateful I retained my Focus for the day", repeat 2 x and sit quietly for 30 seconds focusing on two tasks that you will get done the following day, nothing else. This should take a total of 7 minutes to complete: 1 minute doing the task, 3 minutes to plan your next day (one task to get done), and 3 minutes to write your feelings about completing today's Challenge in your journal.

_____
_____
_____
_____

Day 13

Morning Exercise: First thing in the morning, sit on side of your bed, close your eyes, take three deep breaths (through your nose) and exhale slowly through your mouth, afterwards say, "I am Focused", repeat 2 x and place a pencil directly in front of you and for 30 seconds focus on nothing but the pencil. After 30 seconds (use alarm on your phone or clock), write down what you were feeling and if you were able to only focus on the pencil and nothing else. This should take a total of 2 minutes to complete.

Evening Exercise: Before going to bed, while sitting, take three deep breaths (through your nose) and exhale slowly through your mouth, afterwards say, "I'm grateful I retained my Focus for the day", repeat 2 x and sit quietly for 30 seconds focusing on two tasks that you will get done the following day, nothing else. This should take a total of 7 minutes to complete: 1 minute doing the task, 3 minutes to plan your next day (one task to get done), and 3 minutes to write your feelings about completing today's Challenge in your journal.

_____
_____
_____
_____
_____
_____

Day 14

Morning Exercise: First thing in the morning, sit on side of your bed, close your eyes, take three deep breaths (through your nose) and exhale slowly through your mouth, afterwards say, "I am Focused", repeat 2 x and place a pencil directly in front of you and for 30 seconds focus on nothing but the pencil. After 30 seconds (use alarm on your phone or clock), write down what you were feeling and if you were able to only focus on the pencil and nothing else. This should take a total of 2 minutes to complete.

_____
_____
_____
_____

Evening Exercise: Before going to bed, while sitting, take three deep breaths (through your nose) and exhale slowly through your mouth, afterwards say, "I'm grateful I retained my Focus for the day", repeat 2 x and sit quietly for 30 seconds focusing on two tasks that you will get done the following day, nothing else. This should take a total of 7 minutes to complete: 1 minute doing the task, 3 minutes to plan your next day (one task to get done), and 3 minutes to write your feelings about completing today's Challenge in your journal.

Day 15

Morning Exercise: First thing in the morning, sit on side of your bed, close your eyes, take three deep breaths (through your nose) and exhale slowly through your mouth, afterwards say, "I am Focused", repeat 2 x and sit quietly for 30 seconds focusing what are your top three priorities for the day? After 30 seconds (use alarm on your phone or clock), write down your three top priorities for the week. This should take a total of 2 minutes to complete.

_____

_____

_____

_____

_____

_____

_____

Evening Exercise: Before going to bed, while sitting, take three deep breaths (through your nose) and exhale slowly through your mouth, afterwards say, "I'm grateful I retained my Focus for the day", repeat 2 x and sit quietly for 30 seconds focusing on three tasks that you will get done the following day, nothing else. After 30 seconds (use alarm on your phone or clock), write down your three tasks by order of importance using the TURBO Priority Planning System and what you were feeling. This should take a total of 7 minutes to complete: 1 minute doing the task, 3 minutes to plan your next day (one task to get done), and 3 minutes to write your feelings about completing today's Challenge in your journal.

_____

_____

_____

_____

Day 16

Morning Exercise: First thing in the morning, sit on side of your bed, close your eyes, take three deep breaths (through your nose) and exhale slowly through your mouth, afterwards say, "I am Focused", repeat 2 x and sit quietly for 30 seconds focusing what are your top three priorities for the day? After 30 seconds (use alarm on your phone or clock), write down your three top priorities for the week. This should take a total of 2 minutes to complete.

_____

_____

_____

_____

_____

_____

Evening Exercise: Before going to bed, while sitting, take three deep breaths (through your nose) and exhale slowly through your mouth, afterwards say, "I'm grateful I retained my Focus for the day", repeat 2 x and sit quietly for 30 seconds focusing on three tasks that you will get done the following day, nothing else. After 30 seconds (use alarm on your phone or clock), write down your three tasks by order of importance using the TURBO Priority Planning System and what you were feeling. This should take a total of 7 minutes to complete: 1 minute doing the task, 3 minutes to plan your next day (one task to get done), and 3 minutes to write your feelings about completing today's Challenge in your journal.

_____

_____

_____

_____

_____

_____

Day 17

Morning Exercise: First thing in the morning, sit on side of your bed, close your eyes, take three deep breaths (through your nose) and exhale slowly through your mouth, afterwards say, "I am Focused", repeat 2 x and sit quietly for 30 seconds focusing what are your top three priorities for the day? After 30 seconds (use alarm on your phone or clock), write down your three top priorities for the week. This should take a total of 2 minutes to complete.

Focused-Driven Lifestyle Strategies

Evening Exercise: Before going to bed, while sitting, take three deep breaths (through your nose) and exhale slowly through your mouth, afterwards say, "I'm grateful I retained my Focus for the day", repeat 2 x and sit quietly for 30 seconds focusing on three tasks that you will get done the following day, nothing else. After 30 seconds (use alarm on your phone or clock), write down your three tasks by order of importance using the TURBO Priority Planning System and what you were feeling. This should take a total of 7 minutes to complete: 1 minute doing the task, 3 minutes to plan your next day (one task to get done), and 3 minutes to write your feelings about completing today's Challenge in your journal.

Day 18

Morning Exercise: First thing in the morning, sit on side of your bed, close your eyes, take three deep breaths (through your nose) and exhale slowly through your mouth, afterwards say, "I am Focused", repeat 2 x and sit quietly for 30 seconds focusing what are your top three priorities for the day? After 30 seconds (use alarm on your phone or clock), write down your three top priorities for the week. This should take a total of 2 minutes to complete.

_____

_____

_____

_____

_____

_____

Evening Exercise: Before going to bed, while sitting, take three deep breaths (through your nose) and exhale slowly through your mouth, afterwards say, "I'm grateful I retained my Focus for the day", repeat 2 x and sit quietly for 30 seconds focusing on three tasks that you will get done the following day, nothing else. After 30 seconds (use alarm on your phone or clock), write down your three tasks by order of importance using the TURBO Priority Planning System and what you were feeling. This should take a total of 7 minutes to complete: 1 minute doing the task, 3 minutes to plan your next day (one task to get done), and 3 minutes to write your feelings about completing today's Challenge in your journal.

_____
_____
_____
_____

Day 19

Morning Exercise: First thing in the morning, sit on side of your bed, close your eyes, take three deep breaths (through your nose) and exhale slowly through your mouth, afterwards say, "I am Focused", repeat 2 x and sit quietly for 30 seconds focusing what are your top three priorities for the day? After 30 seconds (use alarm on your phone or clock), write down your three top priorities for the week. This should take a total of 2 minutes to complete.

_____
_____
_____
_____
_____
_____

Evening Exercise: Before going to bed, while sitting, take three deep breaths (through your nose) and exhale slowly through your mouth, afterwards say, "I'm grateful I retained my Focus for the day", repeat 2 x and sit quietly for 30 seconds focusing on three tasks that you will get done the following day, nothing else. After 30 seconds (use alarm on your phone or clock), write down your three tasks by order of importance using the TURBO Priority Planning System and what you were feeling. This should take a total of 7 minutes to complete: 1 minute doing the task, 3 minutes to plan your next day (one task to get done), and 3 minutes to write your feelings about completing today's Challenge in your journal.

_____
_____
_____
_____
_____
_____

Day 20

Morning Exercise: First thing in the morning, sit on side of your bed, close your eyes, take three deep breaths (through your nose) and exhale slowly through your mouth, afterwards say, "I am Focused", repeat 2 x and sit quietly for 30 seconds focusing what are your top three priorities for the day? After 30 seconds (use alarm on your phone or clock), write down your three top priorities for the week. This should take a total of 2 minutes to complete.

_____
_____

Evening Exercise: Before going to bed, while sitting, take three deep breaths (through your nose) and exhale slowly through your mouth, afterwards say, "I'm grateful I retained my Focus for the day", repeat 2 x and sit quietly for 30 seconds focusing on three tasks that you will get done the following day, nothing else. After 30 seconds (use alarm on your phone or clock), write down your three tasks by order of importance using the TURBO Priority Planning System and what you were feeling. This should take a total of 7 minutes to complete: 1 minute doing the task, 3 minutes to plan your next day (one task to get done), and 3 minutes to write your feelings about completing today's Challenge in your journal.

Day 21

Morning Exercise: First thing in the morning, sit on side of your bed, close your eyes, take three deep breaths (through your nose) and exhale slowly through your mouth, afterwards say, "I am Focused", repeat 2 x and sit quietly for 30 seconds focusing what are your top three priorities for the day? After 30 seconds (use alarm on your phone or clock), write down your three top priorities for the week. This should take a total of 2 minutes to complete.

_____
_____
_____
_____
_____
_____
_____

Evening Exercise: Before going to bed, while sitting, take three deep breaths (through your nose) and exhale slowly through your mouth, afterwards say, "I'm grateful I retained my Focus for the day", repeat 2 x and sit quietly for 30 seconds focusing on three tasks that you will get done the following day, nothing else. After 30 seconds (use alarm on your phone or clock), write down your three tasks by order of importance using the TURBO Priority Planning System and what you were feeling. This should take a total of 7 minutes to complete: 1 minute doing the task, 3 minutes to plan your next day (one task to get done), and 3 minutes to write your feelings about completing today's Challenge in your journal.

_____
_____

Day 22

Morning Exercise: First thing in the morning, sit on side of your bed, close your eyes, take three deep breaths (through your nose) and exhale slowly through your mouth, afterwards say, "I am Focused", repeat 2 x and sit quietly for 30 seconds focusing on what you have learned doing this challenge? After 30 seconds (use alarm on your phone or clock), write down what you were feeling and how you have grown through this Challenge so far. This should take a total of 2 minutes to complete.

_____
_____
_____
_____
_____
_____
_____

Evening Exercise: Before going to bed, while sitting, take three deep breaths (through your nose) and exhale slowly through your mouth, afterwards say, "I'm grateful I retained my Focus for the day", repeat 2 x and sit quietly for 30 seconds focusing on three tasks that you will get done the following day, nothing else. After 30 seconds (use alarm on your phone or clock), write down what you were feeling and the names of at least three friends of yours that would benefit from taking the Challenge and inviting them to sign up for the next Get Focused Challenge. Take as much time as you need to list your friends and inviting them to take the challenge.

_____

_____

_____

_____

_____

_____

Day 23

Morning Exercise: First thing in the morning, sit on side of your bed, close your eyes, take three deep breaths (through your nose) and exhale slowly through your mouth, afterwards say, "I am Focused", repeat 2 x and sit quietly for 30 seconds focusing on what you have learned doing this challenge? After 30 seconds (use alarm on your phone or clock), write down what you were feeling and how you have grown through this Challenge so far. This should take a total of 2 minutes to complete.

_____

_____

_____

Evening Exercise: Before going to bed, while sitting, take three deep breaths (through your nose) and exhale slowly through your mouth, afterwards say, "I'm grateful I retained my Focus for the day", repeat 2 x and sit quietly for 30 seconds focusing on three tasks that you will get done the following day, nothing else. After 30 seconds (use alarm on your phone or clock), write down what you were feeling and the names of at least three friends of yours that would benefit from taking the Challenge and inviting them to sign up for the next Get Focused Challenge. Take as much time as you need to list your friends and inviting them to take the challenge.

_____
_____
_____
_____
_____
_____

Day 24

Morning Exercise: First thing in the morning, sit on side of your bed, close your eyes, take three deep breaths (through your nose) and exhale slowly through your mouth, afterwards say, "I am Focused", repeat 2 x and sit quietly for

30 seconds focusing on what you have learned doing this challenge? After 30 seconds (use alarm on your phone or clock), write down what you were feeling and how you have grown through this Challenge so far. This should take a total of 2 minutes to complete.

_____
_____
_____
_____
_____
_____

Evening Exercise: Before going to bed, while sitting, take three deep breaths (through your nose) and exhale slowly through your mouth, afterwards say, "I'm grateful I retained my Focus for the day", repeat 2 x and sit quietly for 30 seconds focusing on three tasks that you will get done the following day, nothing else. After 30 seconds (use alarm on your phone or clock), write down what you were feeling and the names of at least three friends of yours that would benefit from taking the Challenge by purchasing them a copy of this book.

_____
_____
_____

_____
_____
_____

Day 25

Morning Exercise: First thing in the morning, sit on side of your bed, close your eyes, take three deep breaths (through your nose) and exhale slowly through your mouth, afterwards say, "I am Focused", repeat 2 x and sit quietly for 30 seconds focusing on what you have learned doing this challenge? After 30 seconds (use alarm on your phone or clock), write down what you were feeling and how you have grown through this Challenge so far. This should take a total of 2 minutes to complete.

_____
_____
_____
_____
_____

Evening Exercise: Before going to bed, while sitting, take three deep breaths (through your nose) and exhale slowly through your mouth, afterwards say, "I'm grateful I retained my Focus for the day", repeat 2 x and sit quietly for 30 seconds focusing on three tasks that you will get done the following day, nothing else. After 30 seconds (use alarm on your phone or clock), write down what you were feeling and the names of at least three friends of yours that would benefit from taking the Challenge.

_____

_____

_____

_____

_____

Day 26

Morning Exercise: First thing in the morning, sit on side of your bed, close your eyes, take three deep breaths (through your nose) and exhale slowly through your mouth, afterwards say, "I am Focused", repeat 2 x and sit quietly for 30 seconds focusing on what you have learned doing this challenge? After 30 seconds (use alarm on your phone or clock), write down what you were feeling and how you have grown through this Challenge so far. This should take a total of 2 minutes to complete.

_____

_____

_____

_____

Evening Exercise: Before going to bed, while sitting, take three deep breaths (through your nose) and exhale slowly through your mouth, afterwards say, "I'm grateful I retained my Focus for the day", repeat 2 x and sit quietly for 30 seconds focusing on three tasks that you will get done the following day, nothing else. After 30 seconds (use alarm on your phone or clock), write down what you were feeling and the names of at least three friends of yours that would benefit from taking the Challenge and inviting them to sign up for the next Get Focused Challenge. Take as much time as you need to list your friends and inviting them to take the challenge.

_____

_____

_____

_____

_____

_____

Day 27

Morning Exercise: First thing in the morning, sit on side of your bed, close your eyes, take three deep breaths (through your nose) and exhale slowly through your mouth, afterwards say, "I am Focused", repeat 2 x and sit quietly for 30 seconds focusing on what you have learned doing this challenge? After 30 seconds (use alarm on your phone or clock), write down what you were feeling and how you have grown through this Challenge so far. This should take a total of 2 minutes to complete.

_____
_____
_____
_____
_____
_____

Evening Exercise: Before going to bed, while sitting, take three deep breaths (through your nose) and exhale slowly through your mouth, afterwards say, "I'm grateful I retained my Focus for the day", repeat 2 x and sit quietly for 30 seconds focusing on three tasks that you will get done the following day, nothing else. After 30 seconds (use alarm on your phone or clock), write down what you were feeling and the names of at least three friends of yours that would benefit from taking the Challenge and inviting them to sign up for the next Get Focused Challenge. Take as much time as you need to list your friends and inviting them to take the challenge.

_____
_____
_____

Day 28

Morning Exercise: First thing in the morning, sit on side of your bed, close your eyes, take three deep breaths (through your nose) and exhale slowly through your mouth, afterwards say, "I am Focused", repeat 2 x and sit quietly for 30 seconds focusing on what you have learned doing this challenge? After 30 seconds (use alarm on your phone or clock), write down what you were feeling and how you have grown through this Challenge so far. This should take a total of 2 minutes to complete.

_____
_____
_____
_____
_____
_____
_____

Evening Exercise: Before going to bed, while sitting, take three deep breaths (through your nose) and exhale slowly through your mouth, afterwards say, "I'm grateful I retained my Focus for the day", repeat 2 x and sit quietly for 30 seconds focusing on three tasks that you will get done the following day, nothing else. After 30 seconds (use alarm on your phone or clock), write down what you were feeling and the names of at least three friends of yours that would benefit from taking the Challenge.

_____
_____
_____
_____
_____
_____

Day 29

Morning Exercise: First thing in the morning, sit on side of your bed, close your eyes, take three deep breaths (through your nose) and exhale slowly through your mouth, afterwards say, "I am Focused", repeat 2 x and sit quietly for 30 seconds focusing on what you have learned doing this challenge? Focus on one thing you will do today to show you have gained better focus and post a picture in the group of how you will reward yourself for completing the challenge. Today.

_____
_____
_____
_____
_____
_____

Evening Exercise: Before going to bed, while sitting, take three deep breaths (through your nose) and exhale slowly through your mouth, afterwards say, "I'm grateful I retained my Focus for the day", repeat 2 x and sit quietly for 30 seconds focusing on three tasks that you will get done the following day, nothing else. After 30 seconds (use alarm on your phone or clock), write down what you were feeling and the names of at least three friends of yours that would benefit from taking the Challenge and inviting them to sign up for the next Get Focused Challenge. Take as much time as you need to list your friends and inviting them to take the challenge.

_____
_____
_____
_____
_____
_____

Day 30

Morning Exercise: First thing in the morning, sit on side of your bed, close your eyes, take three deep breaths (through your nose) and exhale slowly through your mouth, afterwards say, "I am Focused", repeat 2 x and sit quietly for 30 seconds focusing on what you have learned doing this challenge? Focus on one thing you will do today to show you have gained better focus and post a picture in the group of how you will reward yourself for completing the challenge. Today.

_____
_____
_____
_____
_____
_____

Evening Exercise: Before going to bed, while sitting, take three deep breaths (through your nose) and exhale slowly through your mouth, afterwards say, "I'm grateful I retained my Focus for the day", repeat 2 x and sit quietly for 30 seconds focusing on three tasks that you will get done the following day, nothing else. After 30 seconds (use alarm on your phone or clock), write down what you were feeling and the names of at least three friends of yours that would benefit from taking the Challenge.

_____
_____
_____
_____
_____
_____

Strategy 7: Be Grateful

A challenging lesson to learn in life is to be grateful for all of the many gifts that you have inside of you. I will be the first to acknowledge that I don't always feel grateful until I'm driving down the street and see those that are living in cardboard boxes or begging for a few dollars to get something to eat. Then, it puts things into perspective, "What happened to cause them to be homeless or give up on life? We can argue that they are homeless by choice or begging to fuel their chemical dependency, whatever the circumstance, we are not living their reality. So, whenever you feel down on yourself, remember the song, "Be Grateful" which has a line that says, "There's somebody who would love to be in your shoes." A proverb says, "Gratitude is a reflection of your attitude."

Chapter Ten

Conclusion

As I bring this book to a close, I am confident that I have provided you with the tools needed to live a focused-driven lifestyle. And with that, you also have the knowledge necessary to start organizing your brain, your life and finally feeling on top of your game.

It's a lot to take on board, and of course, it's not going to change overnight. Try to avoid the temptation to force yourself to adopt all these changes right away – instead, take some time out to fix as much as you can and then try to introduce as many positive new habits, and I strongly suggest that you invest in ordering my **Morning Ritual System**. After all, you don't want this to add to your feeling of being overwhelmed! To give you a quick recap, remember to follow this simple action plan that I have provided.

A Day to Rearrange

First, take one day off (or weekend) to deal with as much as you can and thereby give yourself a good fighting chance to get organized. On this day, you're going to accomplish the following:

- Clean and organize your work and living space
- Implement systems – such as keeping clothes to be ironed somewhere useful and how you return phone calls.
- Throw out items to reduce clutter
- Define your focus
- Prioritize social time with the people who are most important to you in life

Moving Forward

From there on, follow these principles to help keep everything in order:

- Ask for help when you need it
- Learn to say "no" when people invite you out, and you just don't have time
- Complete big tasks first at work
- Make plans for the week to reduce decision fatigue
- Add things you need to do to your focus list and treat them– as non-negotiable
- Look after your health and eat for energy
- Schedule time off

- Turn off screens (computer, TV, tablets, mobile devices) an hour before bed

And at work...
- Work on large projects first
- Reduce communication overhead
- Avoid distractions
- VALUE your time and make sure others do too
- Ask for help if you need it
- When you get home from work – Disconnect for a while

Start putting this into practice, give it time and look for more ways that you can organize your work and life. Remember, organization is the foundation of living a focused-driven lifestyle.

Focus your mind, Organize your life and Gain control of your time!

Lyman's Biography

As a child, Lyman A. Montgomery had some physical and mental challenges to overcome; he wore corrective shoes, failed in school, had a severe speech  impediment, was sexually abused by his teacher for three years. As a result of years of abuse, he became withdrawn, emotionally unstable, and spent the next twenty-five years running in circles and accomplishing very little regarding productivity and financial independence.

After missing out on some great business opportunities and continuing to face roadblocks and personal disappointments due to a lack of focus and concentration; Lyman decided to do something different. He learned to clear his mind of distractions and focused his energies on eliminating his debilitating beliefs, and within a few weeks, he saw dramatic results.

Since that time, he has accomplished a lot. He is the founder and president of Focused Driven Lifestyle Coaching, LLC, a company dedicated to working with business leaders and career professionals to remove distractions, set profitable priorities, and take focused action steps to turn priorities into profits. He is a well sought-after conference speaker (over 30 speaking engagements a year) and focus consultant to organizations across the United States. In 2011, he authored the book: <u>Shattered Masks: 7 Masks We Wear</u>. He was recently featured in <u>Business Innovator Magazine</u> and <u>Washington Journal</u>, and won the prestigious Speaking Empire Best Presenter Award and the Empowered Leader Award in 2016.

Professional Credentials

His educational and professional credentials include a Masters in Business Administration; post-graduate training from Harvard University and is currently, pursuing his Ph.D. in Human Resources Management and Leadership. Also, he is a LEAN Six Sigma Black Belt Trainer, Master NLP Practionier; Certified Labor Relations Professional, and National Certified Mediator alone with several other professional certifications.

Lyman believes strongly in creating relationships based on trust. This is done by doing what he commits to doing. If an issue arises, he will be the first to contact you, so you know he is there for you, and you can count on him. He has the credentials and training to take your organization to the next level.

Lyman, believes the key to success is to
Focus...Prioritize...Achieve

Made in the USA
Columbia, SC
30 November 2017